SOCCER★STARS

Pedigree BOOKS

Published by Pedigree Books Limited
The Old Rectory, Matford Lane, Exeter, EX2 4PS.
Under licence from IPC Magazines Limited.

£6.99
S01

Yorke

DWIGHT

TRINIDAD
MAN UNITED

SOCCER★STARS

Dwight On...

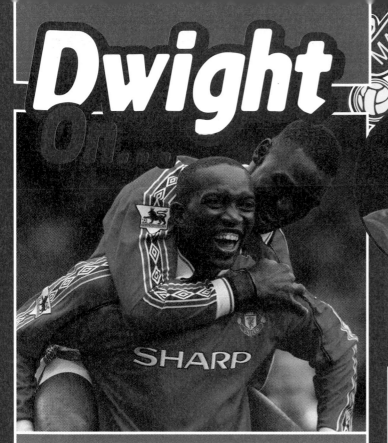

DATAFILE

Name: Dwight Yorke
Born: November 3rd, 1971, in Tobago
Height: 5ft 9ins
Weight: 12st 3lbs
Position: Striker
Clubs played for: Aston Villa, Manchester United
Nickname: Yorkie
Honours: League Cup 1996; FA Premiership 1999, European Cup 1999, FA Cup 1999; Trinidad & Tobago full caps

MAN UNITED

"We have a fantastic squad here. Everyone knows about Giggsy, David Beckham and Paul Scholes but some of the youngsters coming through in the youth team and the reserves are brilliant as well."

THE CHAMPIONS' LEAGUE

"I know that I will never play in the World Cup so the Champions' League is the next best thing. You are against many of the best players in the world and one of the reasons I came to Old Trafford was to play in the competition."

ANDY COLE

"We get on really well off the pitch as well as on it and that has helped our partnership for United. When I first joined the club, Andy took me around Manchester to show me the sights and that helped me settle down straightaway. If you feel comfortable off the park, it helps you on it."

COSTING UNITED A RECORD £12.6 MILLION

"It didn't worry me that the club had paid out so much money for me because I had nothing to do with the fee. It was a dream come true to come to United and all I was worried about was doing my best for the team."

10 things you might not know about....

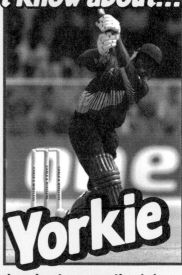

Yorkie

1 Dwight's best friend is West Indies cricketer Brian Lara. The pair grew up together and both had trials for Trinidad's Under-12s football team.

2 When Yorkie joined Man United he became the club's most expensive player at £12.6 million.

3 Dwight scored in five of United's six Champions' League group matches last season. The only one he missed out on was the 1-1 home draw with Bayern Munich.

4 He also hit more than 25 goals for the club last year which makes him one of United's all-time top scorers in a season.

5 Dwight was a good cricketer when he was younger and is also a pretty wicked golfer.

6 When Aston Villa manager John Gregory found out that Yorke wanted to join United he said he wanted to 'shoot him'. Don't worry, he didn't mean it and the two are friends again now!

7 Yorkie has played more than 20 times for Trinidad and Tobago.

8 He scored Aston Villa's third goal in their 3-0 Coca-Cola Cup Final win over Leeds at Wembley in 1996.

9 One of his biggest disappointments is being left out of the Aston Villa side that beat Man United in the 1994 Coca-Cola Cup Final.

10 Dwight scored his first hat-trick for Man United in their 6-2 win at Leicester on January 16th, 1999.

Cool moment

MARCH 3, 1999...OLD TRAFFORD...MAN UNITED V INTER MILAN....CHAMPIONS' LEAGUE Q-F

Two headed goals from the United striker gave The Reds a 2-0 first leg lead. David Beckham swung over an inch perfect cross on six minutes for Yorkie to head past goalie Gianluca Pagliuca, and on the stroke of half-time the Trinidad star struck again as United built up a winning lead.

DATAFILE

Name: David Ginola
Born: January 25th, 1967 in Gassin, France
Height: 5ft 11ins
Weight: 11st 10lbs
Position: Winger
Clubs played for: Toulon, Racing Paris, Brest, Paris St. Germain (all France), Newcastle, Tottenham
Normal shirt number: 14

David On....

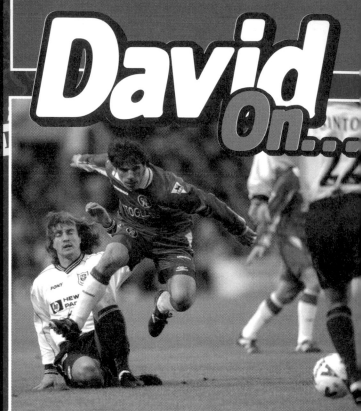

HIS HERO AS A YOUNGSTER
"The Dutch star from the 1970s, Johan Cruyff, was my idol. I used to watch what he did in matches and try to copy his skills. When I played in games, I used to try and think what Johan would do, then do the same."

PLAYING SKILFUL FOOTBALL
"The most important thing to me when I play football is to entertain the fans. That is why I play the game. They pay good money to come and watch and they should be given a show."

TIPS FOR SOCCERSTARS READERS
"Practice your skills and don't be afraid to try out different things. If they don't come off, try again. Listen and you will learn. But the most important thing is to make sure you enjoy playing the game."

BERGKAMP, ZOLA AND CO
"Players like Bergkamp and Zola are world class, there is no doubt about that. They have made the Premiership a better league. In England now, you have many of the best performers in the world playing. That makes it so exciting for the fans."

10 things you might not know about.... Ginola

1. David's first trophy in England was the Worthington Cup with Spurs in 1999. They beat Leicester 1-0 in the Final.
2. He was voted Footballer of the Year by both the PFA and the Football Writers for 1998-99.
3. His dad is Italian and used to play professional football himself.
4. David enjoys golf and tennis and also plays 'pub games' like darts and dominoes.
5. Ginola loves motor racing. He is a big fan of Jacques Villeneuve and Jean Alesi
6. He enjoys all types of music and has nearly 1,000 CDs in his collection.
7. In his summer holidays, David is likely to head for the beaches in the South of France, although one day he would like to visit the Amazon jungle.
8. As well as Dutch legend Johan Cruyff, David was also a big fan of Michel Platini, a great French player from the 1980s.
9. He fell out with Eric Cantona after the former Man United star blamed Ginola for costing France a place in the 1994 World Cup. David gave away the ball in the last seconds of the deciding qualifier against Bulgaria and they broke away to score the winner.
10. He has done TV adverts for two of his greatest loves - cars and his hair!

Cool moment

MARCH 16, 1999...OAKWELL...BARNSLEY V TOTTENHAM....FA CUP Q-F...

With the score at 0-0, the brilliant French international picked the ball up just inside his own half and dribbled around four Barnsley defenders before calmly slotting the ball into the net for one of the goals of the season.

Ginola

DAVID

FRANCE
TOTTENHAM

SOCCER★STARS

DATAFILE

Name: Paul Gascoigne
Born: May 27th, 1967 in Gateshead
Height: 5ft 10in
Weight: 11st 10lbs
Position: Midfielder
Clubs played for: Newcastle, Tottenham, Lazio (Italy), Rangers, Middlesbrough
Nickname: Gazza
Normal shirt number: 8

10 things you might not know about.... Gazza

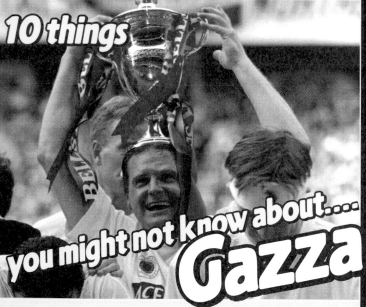

1. Paul had a chart hit in 1991 with the song 'Fog on the Tyne' recorded with Geordie band, Lindisfarne

2. He became a national hero at the 1990 World Cup and was voted one of the best 11 players in the world during the tournament.

3. His popularity in this country went up even further after he cried at the end of the Semi-Final defeat by Germany in the competition.

4. He suffered cruciate ligament damage in the FA Cup Final win over Nottingham Forest in 1991 and had to leave the pitch after only 15 minutes. That was his last game for Spurs.

5. Gazza's first goal for Italian club Lazio was a last minute equaliser in the local derby against Roma and made him an instant hero with the club's fans.

6. He appeared with Gary Lineker in a TV advert for Walker's Crisps.

7. He once dressed up as Father Christmas and entertained the shoppers at Selfridges in London.

8. Gazza loves Mars Bars but had to cut down on eating them because they were making him gain weight.

9. He scored a hat-trick for Rangers at Aberdeen to clinch the Scottish title on the last day of 1995-96.

10. He has always been a joker in the dressing-room and one of his pranks is to cut off the toes of his team-mates' socks.

Gascoigne

Gazza On...

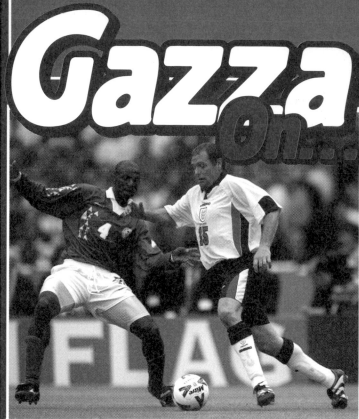

LARKING ABOUT
"I will never change. I have always tried to make people laugh, even when I was a kid. Sometimes I know I should be on my best behaviour and I have tried but that's just the way I am."

PLAYING FOOTBALL AS A KID
"I used to play football all the time, even when I should have been doing my homework and things like that. My mates and I would always be out in the street or down the park. I played for a boys' club as well."

EATING CHOCOLATE AND BURGERS
"It is not very clever for a player to eat chocolate and burgers now. In the old days, when I was a youngster, no-one minded so much but now footballers have pretty strict diets."

PLAYING FOR ENGLAND
"I used to dream about playing for England so to put on a white shirt for the first time was very special. It was the lowest point of my career when I was left out of the squad for France 98."

Cool moment

APRIL 14, 1991....WEMBLEY...
ARSENAL V TOTTENHAM...FA CUP SEMI-FINAL

Gazza struck one of the greatest goals in Wembley history in this Semi-Final showdown. Fully 30 yards out, he smashed a brilliant, swerving free-kick past David Seaman to help Spurs to a 3-1 victory.

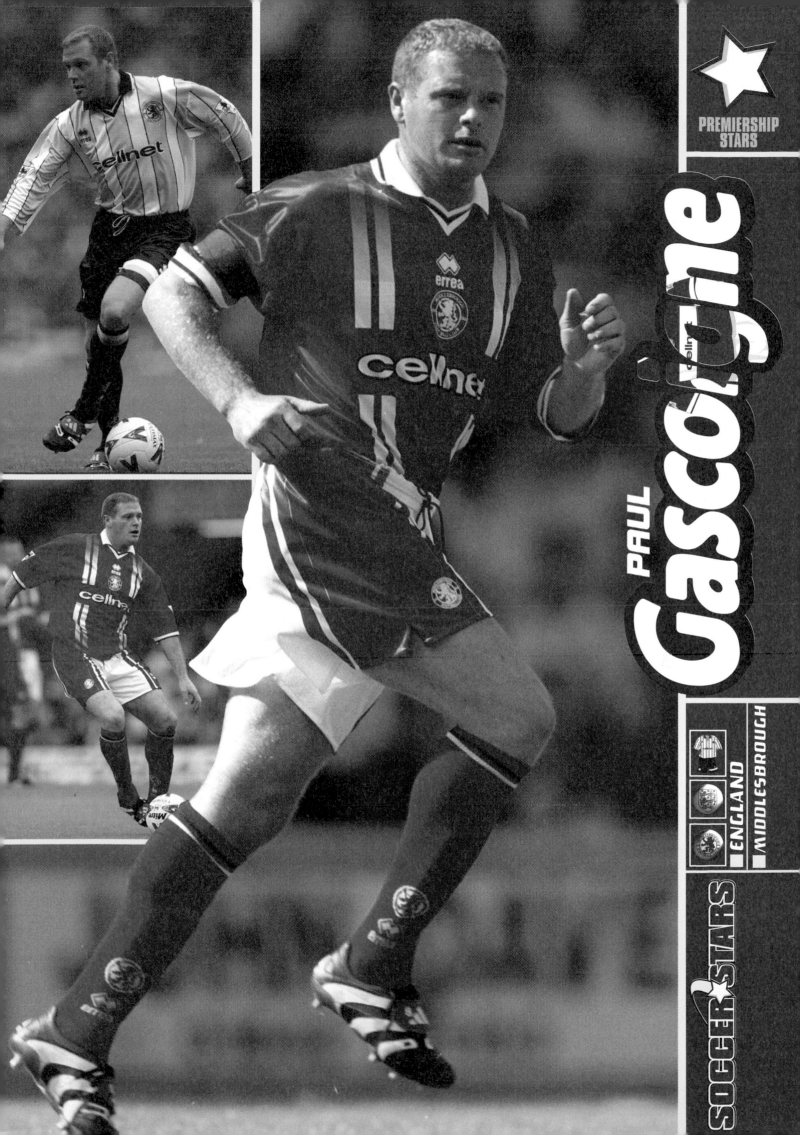

PREMIERSHIP STARS

PAUL **Gascoigne**

ENGLAND
MIDDLESBROUGH

SOCCER STARS

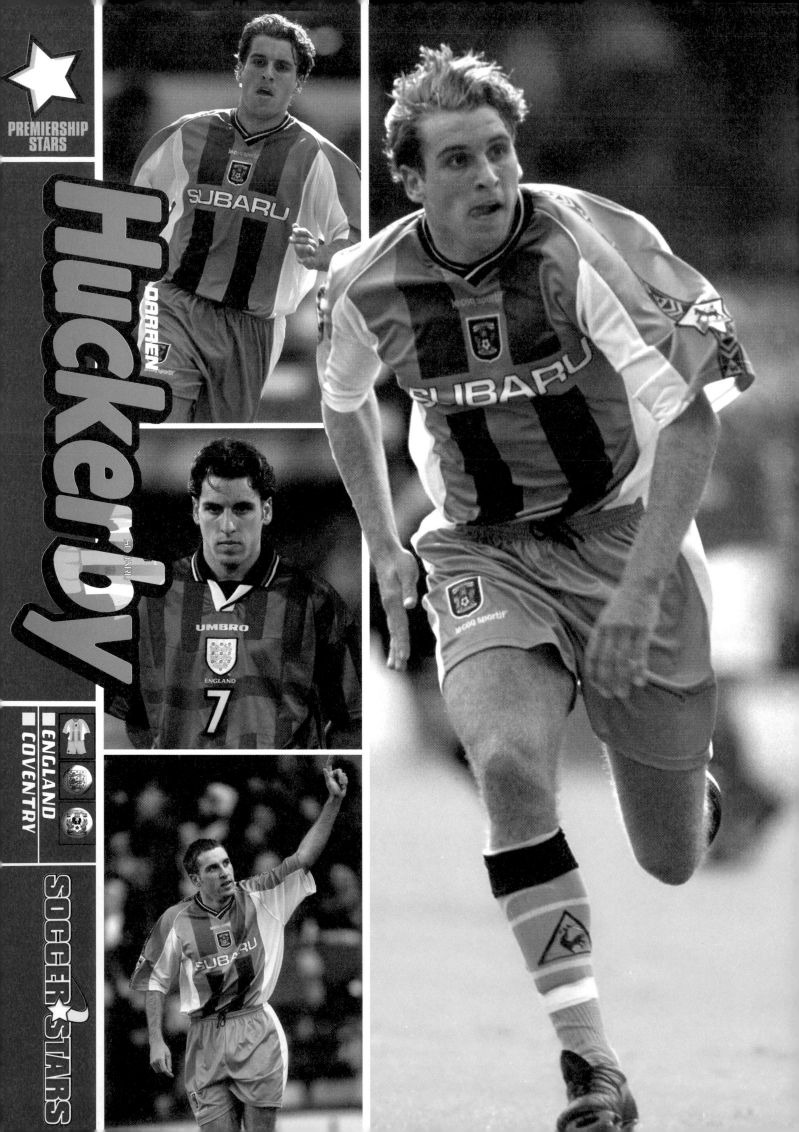

DARREN

Huckerby

SUBARU

UMBRO

ENGLAND

7

■ ENGLAND
■ COVENTRY

SOCCER★STARS

Darren On...

DATAFILE

Name: Darren Carl Huckerby
Born: April 23rd, 1976 in Nottingham
Height: 5ft 10in
Weight: 11st 12lb
Position: Striker
Clubs played for: Lincoln, Newcastle, Millwall (on loan), Coventry
Nickname: Hucks

AMBITIONS IN FOOTBALL

"I want to play for the very best teams that I can and to win every honour that's going - that's all! I'd also love to get into the England squad. That is a great ambition of mine. To represent your country is the highest honour you can get as a professional footballer."

HERO WORSHIP

"I enjoyed watching quite a few players, but mainly strikers. Gary Lineker and Peter Beardsley were big favourites of mine, but I liked studying anyone who was good in front of goal."

TOUGH DEFENDERS

"Tottenham's Sol Campbell is always very difficult to play against. He's big and strong and I always have a battle with him. So I don't look forward to playing against Spurs!"

LEAVING NEWCASTLE

"I just had to get away from Newcastle because I was never playing in the first-team. Nobody really knew what I could do or how I could play, so going to Coventry brought me to everyone's attention. That's all it was really: to play some serious games."

Cool moment

APRIL 25, 1998...ELLAND ROAD... LEEDS V COVENTRY... FA PREMIERSHIP...

A fantastic display of speed and strength saw Darren score his first ever professional hat-trick. Twice in the first-half Jimmy Hasselbaink put Leeds ahead, and twice Darren struck back. In the second-half, speed merchant Huckerby pounced again in this thrilling 3-3 draw.

10 things you might not know about... Huckerby

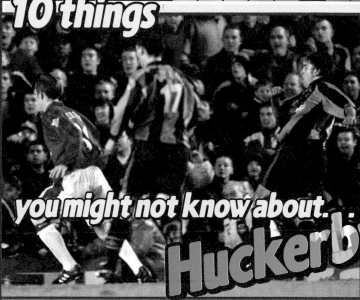

1. Darren scored an amazing solo goal against Manchester United in 1997-98 to win BBC TV's 'Goal of the Month' award for December 1997.

2. Huckerby signed a new four-year contract with Coventry in March 1998.

3. His younger brother, Scott, is a forward for Telford in the Nationwide Football Conference.

4. Darren's pro career began with Lincoln City, where he signed from trainee on July 14th, 1993.

5. He transferred to Newcastle in November 1995 - but was released within a year by the Magpies then manager, Kevin Keegan.

6. After a brief spell on loan at Millwall the lightning fast wide man joined Coventry in November 1996 - for a cool £1 million. Not a bad price for a Reserve player!

7. A survey showed that he was caught offside more than any of his team-mates in the 1998-99 season.

8. His England Under-21 debut came as a substitute against Italy in a European Championship qualifying game at Ashton Gate, Bristol in February 1997. England won 1-0.

9. If he wasn't a footballer, he would probably have tried his luck as a firefighter. "I like action and excitement, so something like a fireman would be a pretty cool job," explains Darren.

10. Born and bred in Nottingham, Huckerby grew up as a huge Notts County fan.

NICOLAS Anelka

FRANCE
ARSENAL

SOCCER STARS

Nicolas On...

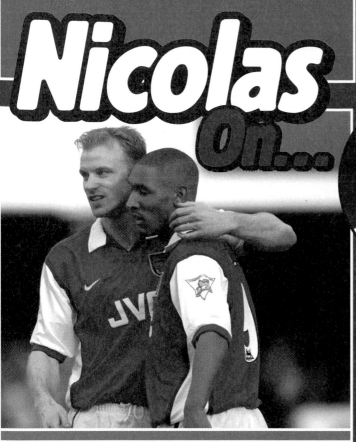

DATAFILE

Name: Nicolas Anelka
Born: March 14th, 1979 in Versailles, France
Height: 5ft 11in
Weight: 12st 3lb
Position: Striker
Clubs played for: Paris St. Germain (France), Arsenal
Honours: FA Premiership 1998; FA Cup 1998; France Youth, Under-21 and full caps

SCORING IN THE 1998 FA CUP FINAL

"That goal against Newcastle was my greatest moment as an Arsenal player. I used to dream about scoring in a Cup Final when I was a kid and when the ball hit the net, it was a magic feeling. I knew all my friends and family would be watching the game in France as well."

ARSENE WENGER

"I owe so much to my manager at Arsenal, Arsene Wenger. He has taught me about the game and gave me a chance at Highbury at a young age. He proved just what a good manager he is by taking us to the double in his first full season in England."

PLAYING ALONGSIDE BERGKAMP

"It is a delight to be in the same side as Dennis. He creates so many chances for me with his passing and skill. Defenders can't get near him. He always seems to be one step ahead of everyone else."

SCORING GOALS

"It is what every striker is paid to do. I struggled at the start for Arsenal but last season I was top scorer and that gave me great satisfaction. I have never doubted my ability though."

10 things you might not know about.... Anelka

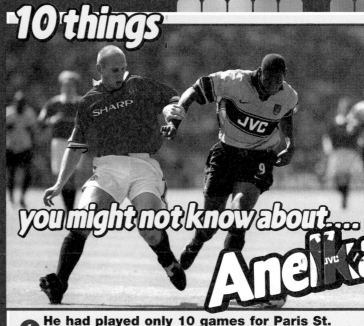

1. He had played only 10 games for Paris St. Germain before Arsenal signed him, aged 17.
2. Nicolas is very shy and quiet off the pitch. He says he misses his friends in France.
3. He has played for France at Youth and Under-21 levels as well as for the senior side.
4. Anelka scored both goals for France in their 2-0 win against England at Wembley in February 1999. Marking him that day was his Arsenal skipper, Tony Adams.
5. He is short-sighted and wears contact lenses when he is playing.
6. His manager, Arsene Wenger, says he wouldn't sell him - even for £20m.
7. As a kid back home in France, he was nicknamed the 'French Maradona'.
8. Arsenal paid out only £500,000 to Paris St. Germain for Anelka.
9. Man United defender Jaap Stam rates Nicolas as the most difficult opponent he has faced in the Premiership.
10. Anelka says the reason he doesn't say much to the press and TV in this country is that he hasn't achieved anything yet.

Cool moment

MAY 16, 1998...WEMBLEY...
ARSENAL V NEWCASTLE...FA CUP FINAL

The Gunners striker escaped the Newcastle offside trap after 69 minutes and galloped clear before firing past Shay Given. Anelka's goal sealed a 2-0 win for his side and completed the League and FA Cup double.

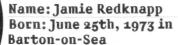

Name: Jamie Redknapp
Born: June 25th, 1973 in Barton-on-Sea
Height: 6ft
Weight: 12st 10lb
Position: Midfielder
Clubs played for: Bournemouth, Liverpool
Nickname: Redders
Honours: League Cup 1995; England Schools, Youth, Under-21, 'B' and full caps

10 things

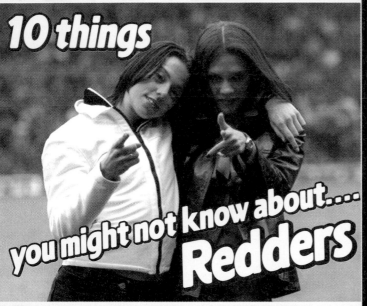

you might not know about..... Redders

● He went on a two-week trial at Liverpool when he was 15 and was tipped by then boss Kenny Dalglish as having a big future.

● Jamie was part of a group of young Liverpool players given the label 'The Spice Boys' in 1996.

● He played under his dad Harry's management at Bournemouth, making his debut as a 17-year-old.

● In the summer of 1998 Jamie married the pop singer Lousie Nurding.

● Redders is also friends with Mel C from the Spice Girls. She is a big Liverpool fan.

● He had mixed fortunes in England's Euro 96 match with Scotland at Wembley. Coming on as a half-time sub, he ran the game for 25 minutes and helped his side take the lead before suffering an ankle injury that put him out of action for six months.

● One of his biggest disappointments was missing the 1998 World Cup through injury.

● Redders was once voted the best looking player in football by readers of Smash Hits magazine.

● Jamie, Jason McAteer and Phil Babb have appeared on a video for one of Louise's records.

● He has added to his wages as a footballer by doing a bit of part-time modelling.

Jamie On...

BEING MARRIED TO LOUISE
"I enjoy spending time at home or going out for a meal with my wife. Sometimes it gets hard to have a private life because we are both in the spotlight, but generally it is not too bad and we see as much of each other as we can."

PLAYING FOR LIVERPOOL
"I have always wanted to play for them. They are one of the biggest clubs in Europe and it is an honour to put on the red shirt. The fans are brilliant and now we have to give them the success they deserve."

HAVING A DAD AS A MANAGER
"I get on really well with my dad, Harry, who is manager at West Ham. He tries to watch as many of my games as he can and I speak to him more than anyone really - apart from Louise of course."

COMPETING IN MIDFIELD
"You have to be willing to get stuck in during a game because that's the way it is in midfield nowadays. Players like Roy Keane, Manu Petit and Patrick Vieira can all pass the ball but they can all dig in as well and that's what makes them the best."

Cool moment

JANUARY 10, 1998... ANFIELD... LIVERPOOL v WIMBLEDON... FA PREMIERSHIP

Wimbledon travelled to Anfield with a tremendous record of no defeats there in six games, but two Redknapp blockbusters ended that run. Dons' 'keeper Neil Sullivan was left stunned by strikes from 25 and 30 yards that ripped into his net as Liverpool won 2-0.

JAMIE

RedKnapp

ENGLAND
LIVERPOOL

SOCCER★STARS

DATAFILE

Name: Jerral Floyd Hasselbaink
Born: March 27th, 1972 in Paramaribo, Surinam
Height: 6ft 2in
Weight: 13st 5lb
Position: Striker
Clubs played for:
Campomairorense, Boavista (both Portugal), Leeds United
Nickname: Jimmy

10 things you might not know about.... Hasselbaink

1 His real name is Jerral but everyone knows him as Jimmy.

2 He scored his first goal for Leeds on his debut, a 1-1 draw with Arsenal, on August 9th, 1997.

3 In his one and only year at Boavista, he scored 20 goals in 29 League games and finished as one of the top scorers in Portugal.

4 He has been timed as having the hardest shot at Leeds, hitting the ball at more than 80mph.

5 Jimmy was the joint top scorer in the Premiership last season with Dwight Yorke and Michael Owen. All three players scored 18 goals.

6 Surinam-born Jimmy made his debut for Holland when he came on as a substitute against Cameroon in a 0-0 draw in May 1998.

7 He didn't have to wait too long for his first goal - it came in his very next match, a 5-1 win over Paraguay in Eindhoven.

8 Leeds paid out what has proved a bargain £2 million to Portuguese club Boavista for Jimmy in 1997.

9 In his first season at Elland Road, he was voted Player of the Year.

10 Jimmy regularly plays charity matches to raise money for the people of Surinam and the nearby island of Aruba.

Jimmy On...

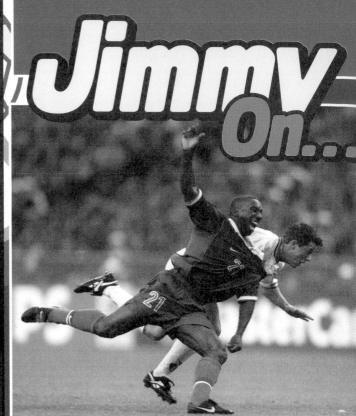

COMING TO ENGLAND
"It was a bit of a shock when Leeds came in for me while I was in Portugal with Boavista, although I had heard of their interest. But the challenge of playing in the Premiership - against so many top players - was just what I was looking for at the time and I didn't take long to make up my mind."

SCORING GOALS
"That is my job. I have always been confident of scoring goals and when I came to England, it had been on the back of a very good year for me at Boavista. I knew that I could repeat that form at Elland Road because I was surrounded by such good players."

LEEDS' YOUNGSTERS
"We have some terrific young players at this club and if they maintain their improvement, we will definitely be Championship challengers for a few years to come. They are gaining experience all the time and that will make them even better players."

WORLD CUP FOOTBALL
"Playing for Holland in France 98 was one of the highlights of my career. Every player dreams of representing his country."

Cool moment

APRIL 3, 1999...ELLAND ROAD...
LEEDS V NOTT'M FOR...FA PREMIERSHIP
Championship-chasing Leeds were struggling to break down Forest until the powerful Dutchman got the ball deep in his own half. He shrugged off three challenges on a 60 yard run before a blockbuster of a shot ended in the Forest net from 30 yards. Totally cool!

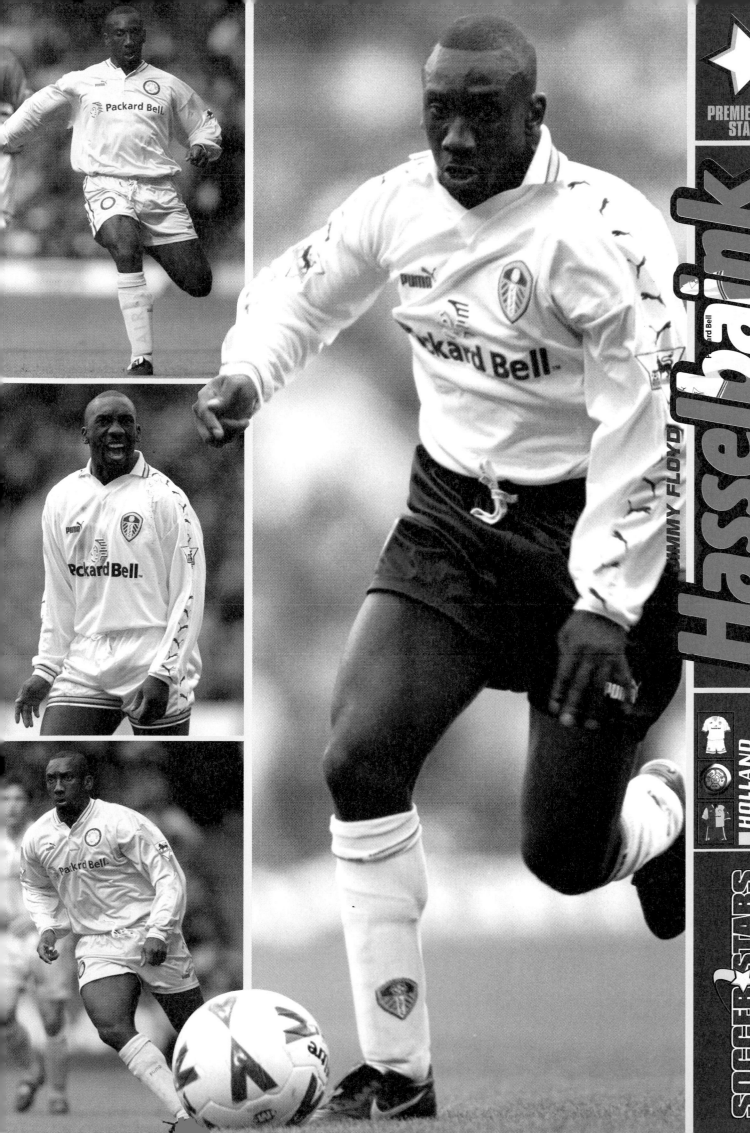

JIMMY FLOYD

Hasselbaink

HOLLAND
LEEDS

TORE ANDRE

FLO

AUTOGLAS

■ NORWAY
■ CHELSEA

SOCCER★STARS

Tore Andre On...

DATAFILE

Name: Tore Andre Flo
Born: June 15th, 1973 in Strin, Norway
Height: 6ft 4in
Weight: 13st 8lb
Position: Striker
Clubs played for: Sogndal, Tromso, Brann (all Norway), Chelsea
Nickname: Flonaldo
Honours: League Cup 1998; Euro Cup-Winners' Cup 1998; Norway full caps

PLAYING ALONGSIDE ZOLA

"It is absolutely brilliant to have someone as good as Gianfranco alongside you. He has so much skill and imagination and is always likely to set up a goal chance for you. He is world-class and I'd like to think we have developed a good understanding."

THE PREMIERSHIP

"The Premiership is a very hard league to play in because there are so many good teams. It is exciting for the fans and having so many great players makes it one of the best leagues - if not the best - in the world."

BEING A SUCCESS AT CHELSEA

"It was hard for me last season because I was out of the side at the start and then got a bad injury. When you have been on the sidelines for a while, it takes you time to get back to the pace of the game. But I was pleased with the way things went in the end and I'm determined to be a big part of Chelsea's future."

CHELSEA'S MAIN RIVALS

"Arsenal and Man United are two excellent sides. United have amazing depth and Arsenal never know when they are beaten."

Cool moment

JUNE 23, 1998...MARSEILLE...NORWAY V BRAZIL...WORLD CUP FINALS

Norway were only eight minutes away from going out of the World Cup - then Flo took centre stage. He scored his side's equaliser against Brazil and then, in the final minute, was hauled down for a penalty that gave his team a famous 2-1 win over the world champions.

10 things you might not know about..... Flo

1. After scoring twice for Norway against Brazil in 1997 he earned the nickname 'Flonaldo' for his efforts.

2. Tore comes from a successful family. His older brother, Jostein, and cousin, Harvard, are also both Norwegian internationals.

3. His favourite food is Norwegian salmon.

4. Tore is a big fan of computer games, especially ones involving motor racing.

5. He likes the music of Celine Dion.

6. Flo scored just three minutes after coming on as a substitute for Mark Hughes on his Chelsea debut in a 3-2 defeat at Coventry in August 1997.

7. For his pre-match meal he has spaghetti bolognaise.

8. He rates Man United's Ronny Johnsen as his most difficult opponent.

9. Flo says that the second goal he scored in Chelsea's 2-1 Quarter-Final win in Real Betis in the 1997-98 European Cup-Winners' Cup was the best strike of his career - so far.

10. He scored a hat-trick in Chelsea's 6-1 win at Tottenham in December 1997.

Quiz

What do you remember

THE ANSWERS TO THESE QUESTIONS CAN ALL BE FOUND IN OUR PREM STARS SECTION.

1. WHICH CLUB DID DWIGHT YORKE LEAVE TO JOIN MAN UNITED?

2. DID NICOLAS ANELKA SCORE IN THE 1998 FA CUP FINAL?

3. JAMIE REDKNAPP IS MARRIED TO WHICH FAMOUS POP STAR?

4. DAVID GINOLA LEFT MIDDLESBROUGH OR NEWCASTLE TO JOIN TOTTENHAM?

5. PAUL GASCOIGNE'S LAST GAME FOR TOTTENHAM WAS THE 1990 FA CUP FINAL. TRUE OR FALSE?

6. FOR WHICH COUNTRY DOES CHELSEA'S TORE ANDRE FLO PLAY?

SOCCER STARS

QUIZ Time No.1

Link 'em up

BELOW ARE THE BADGES AND STRIPS OF SIX PREMIERSHIP CLUBS FROM LAST SEASON. JUST LINK THEM UP BY DRAWING A LINE FROM THE BADGE TO THE MATCHING STRIP.

WORDSEARCH

Hidden in the wordsearch are the names of 12 Premiership players. They can be found in the grid below vertically, horizontally, diagonally or even backwards. We've found the first one for you. Can you spot the rest?

Here are the players to look out for:

Lee BOWYER Sol CAMPBELL Robbie FOWLER David GINOLA Emile HESKEY Julian JOACHIM Frank LAMPARD Dan PETRESCU David SEAMAN Alan SHEARER Teddy SHERINGHAM Patrick VIEIRA

HAPPY HUNTING!

.	H	B	O	W	Y	E	R	E	L	W	O	F
(	T	O	R	K	I	A	C	E	A	L	C	M
/\	V	V	H	E	L	C	E	A	M	A	M	B
C	W	I	S	X	L	L	E	B	P	M	A	C
H	M	E	E	O	N	O	N	R	A	S	H	E
I	T	P	A	I	U	C	S	E	R	T	E	P
N	C	A	M	P	R	R	L	L	D	N	S	A
/\	O	O	A	P	E	A	K	A	Y	G	E	Y
N	S	M	N	R	S	L	A	R	J	T	K	E
L	E	R	A	Y	G	O	E	R	T	E	R	K
F	E	E	D	I	N	N	N	D	S	O	O	S
S	H	L	S	K	J	I	E	R	T	O	Y	E
S	H	E	R	I	N	G	H	A	M	I	Y	H

SOCCER STARS

Personal file

> Born: In Chester, on December 14th, 1979
> Height: 5ft 9in
> Weight: 10st 4lb
> Family: My dad's called Terry, and my mum is Sue
> Home: I live in Hawarden, north Wales, where I am having a house built quite near to my parents
> Honours: FA Youth Cup 1996; England Schools, Youth, Under-21 and full caps, PFA Young Player of the Year 1998

When I was A boy

WHO DID YOU SUPPORT AS A LAD?
Believe it or not, I was an Everton fan! I actually played for their youth sides a few times and my dad played for them as well.

WHAT WAS YOUR FIRST KIT?
I can't really remember - I played for loads of different teams. I would have had an Everton one, though.

WHO WAS YOUR CHILDHOOD HERO?
The Everton and England striker Gary Lineker - he made scoring goals look so easy.

WHAT WERE YOU LIKE AT SCHOOL?
Not too bad, really. I passed all my GCSE's, which was an important thing for me.

My Favourite...

MEAL: Nothing in particular, but I enjoy a meal out with my family and girlfriend.
OTHER SPORT: I'm very keen on golf. My game isn't too bad. I often play a round with my dad after training.
OTHER PLAYER: I used to pretend to be Gazza when I was kicking around with my mates. I've got a lot of respect for Alan Shearer, while Ian Rush and Robbie Fowler at Liverpool have also been an inspiration to me.
GROUND: It's hard to beat playing in front of a packed house at Anfield or Wembley.
GOAL: One I got for England Schoolboys against Scotland. They had just scored and I got the ball from our kick-off and ran and ran and ran - when I got to the edge of the box I just smashed it and it went in the top corner. I don't think I'll ever score a better goal than that one!

Talking Football

WHICH OPPONENT ALWAYS GIVES YOU A TOUGH TIME?
They are all good at the top level. Sometimes you look at a defender and think "he's a big lad", but you try and find their weak spots. If I had to pick one out I'd go for Sol Campbell.

WHO HAS BEEN THE BIGGEST INFLUENCE ON YOUR CAREER?
It's a toss up between Liverpool's Youth Development Officer, Steve Heighway, and my dad. He used to be a professional himself and has been to almost every game I've ever played.

WHAT'S BEEN YOUR BIGGEST FOOTBALL THRILL?
Every time I run out onto the pitch with my team I get a thrill, whether it's Liverpool, England or whoever. And scoring goals of course, that's what it's all about for me. But getting called up to the England squad for the first time was something else. I was out playing golf when I found out, and the news quite put me off my stroke!

MILLS
2

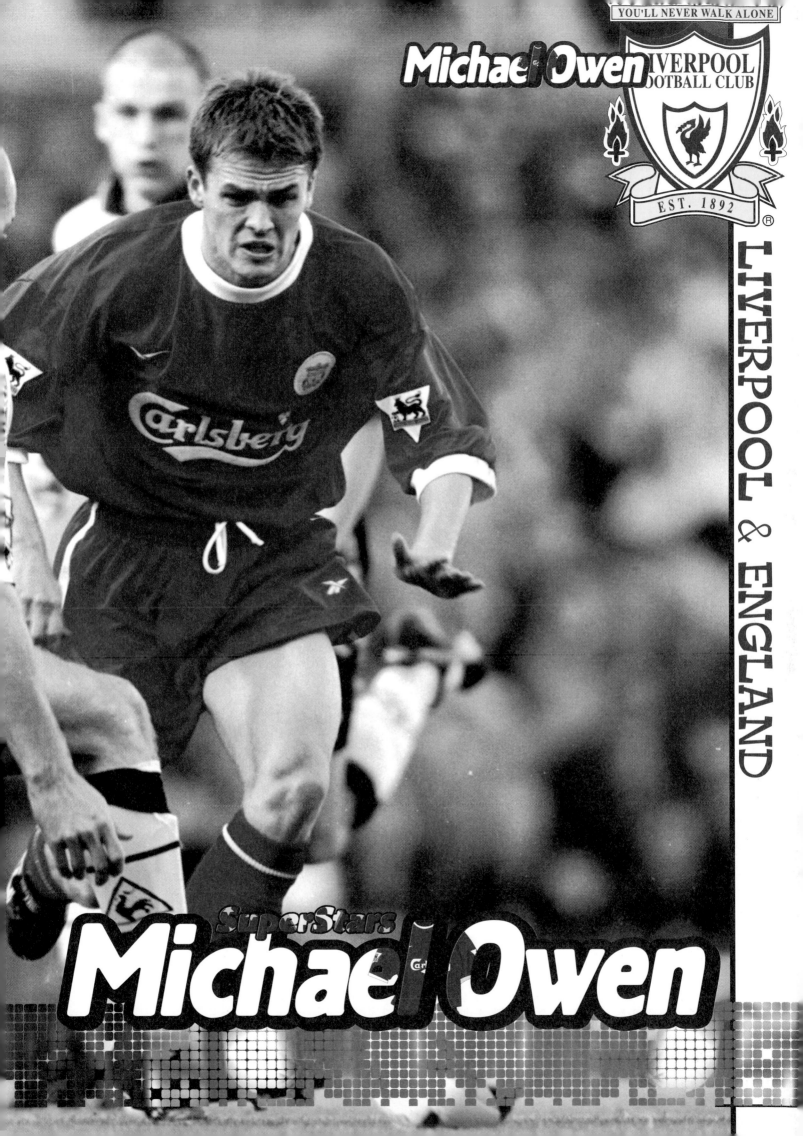

Michael Owen IVERPOOL OOTBALL CLUB

YOU'LL NEVER WALK ALONE

EST. 1892

LIVERPOOL & ENGLAND

SuperStars
Michael Owen

Personal file

Born: In Cardiff, on November 29th, 1973
Height: 5ft 11in
Weight: 10st 9lb
Honours: Super Cup 1991; League Cup 1992;
FA Premiership 1993, 1994, 1996, 1997, 1999;
Charity Shield 1993, 1994, 1996, 1997; FA Cup
1994, 1996, 1999; European Cup 1999; England
Schools caps; Wales Youth, Under-21 and Full
caps; PFA Young Player of the Year 1992, 1993

When I was A boy

WHO DID YOU SUPPORT AS A LAD?
United, of course! I remember that I hated Liverpool at the time because they won everything. It was just jealousy, and it's the same now when people say they hate United.

WHAT WAS YOUR FIRST KIT?
A United one - even though I played for City as a kid. I even slept under a Man United duvet!

WHO WAS YOUR CHILDHOOD HERO?
I loved watching all the really skilful players - still do really. People like Glenn Hoddle or Gazza.

WHAT WERE YOU LIKE AT SCHOOL?
Hopeless, to be honest - I should have concentrated more.

My Favourite...

OTHER SPORT: My dad played rugby league at professional level so I have always had an interest in that.

HOLIDAY DESTINATION: I went to Antigua once and that was great.

GOAL: The one I got against Arsenal in the FA Cup Semi-Final last season is probably the best I have ever scored, especially as it was so important.

POLITICIAN: I met Nelson Mandela when United went on tour to South Africa a few years back and was very impressed by him.

POSITION: I'd have to say winger. It's the position I know best and feel most comfortable in.

GROUND: I love turning out at places like Anfield and Elland Road...anywhere there's a bit of needle. I love that. It really inspires me.

Talking Football

ARE YOU GLAD THAT DAVID BECKHAM'S AROUND TO TAKE SOME OF THE MEDIA PRESSURE OFF YOU THESE DAYS?
Yes, I love it! A few of the younger lads have come in and grabbed the spotlight - people like Becks and Paul Scholes - and I'm happy with that. It allows me to get on with my game a bit more.

WHAT'S IT LIKE PLAYING FOR WALES?
I think when Wales has a full team we are a pretty good side. But if we get injuries in key areas, then we haven't got a big strong squad like other countries have.

YOU'VE HAD CONSTANT SUCCESS SINCE YOU WERE ABOUT 14 - DOESN'T IT GET A BIT BORING?
Not for me, I think you get more enjoyment each time you win something. Each time we win the Premiership, for example, it's more satisfying and you want more and more.

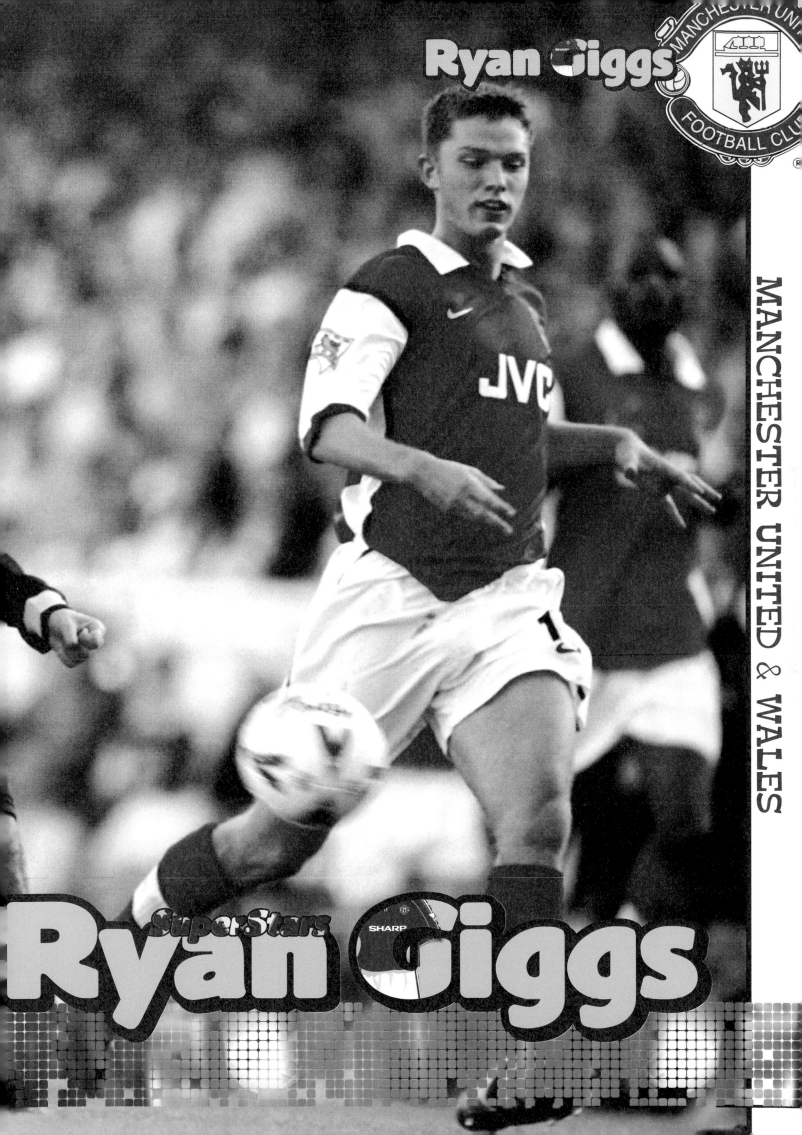

Ryan Giggs

MANCHESTER UNITED & WALES

SuperStars Ryan Giggs

Personal file

Born: In Paisley, Scotland, on August 7th, 1969
Height: 5ft 11in
Weight: 10st 6lb
Family: I am married to Monica and we have a daughter, Kira, and a son called Christopher
Home: We live in a village called Houston
Honours: Scottish Cup 1987, Champions' League 1997, Scottish Championship 1998, Scottish Coca-Cola Cup 1998

When I was A boy

WHO DID YOU SUPPORT AS A BOY?
My local side, St Mirren

WHAT WAS YOUR FIRST KIT?
Man City's away kit from the mid-1970s. It was white with a blue and red diagonal stripe across it.

WHO WAS YOUR CHILDHOOD HERO?
I was a big fan of Kenny Dalglish, but I can't say I had a real hero.

WHAT WERE YOU LIKE AT SCHOOL?
I was quite good at woodwork. Science was my worst subject, I was absolutely hopeless at it.

My Favourite...

MEAL: Pasta
TV PROGRAMME: I love watching Only Fools and Horses.
OTHER SPORT: Golf, although I don't play much.
OTHER SPORTING STAR: Boxer Mike Tyson. His commitment and determination were amazing.
MUSIC: I like all types of music but my favourite album at the moment is George Michael's Greatest Hits.
COMPUTER GAME: My son Christoper will no doubt start playing them soon so I will have to pick up some tips!
FILM: I watched Mel Gibson star in Braveheart and thought that was excellent. He is a very good actor.

Talking Football

WHICH PLAYER DO YOU MOST ADMIRE?
The German defender Jurgen Kohler. He's a great player and played a massive part in his country's success down the years.

WHAT IS THE BEST GOAL YOU HAVE SCORED?
I cracked in one from 20 yards against Rangers in the 1997-98 season and that was pretty special.

WHAT IS THE BEST GOAL YOU HAVE SEEN SCORED?
Marco Van Basten scored a brilliant goal for Holland against Russia in the 1988 European Championship Final. He volleyed the ball in from near the touchline. Incredible.

WHAT HAS BEEN YOUR MOST MEMORABLE GAME?
The Champions' League Final for Borussia Dortmund when we beat Juventus in 1997 was great and to play in the opening match of the 1998 World Cup for Scotland against Brazil was an honour.

HOW DISAPPOINTING WAS IT TO LOSE OUT TO RANGERS LAST YEAR IN THE LEAGUE?
Very. There is great rivalry between the clubs, obviously, but we gave them a head start and could never catch up. To lose the League at home to them was a massive disappointment for us as well.

Paul Lambert

CELTIC & SCOTLAND

Paul Lambert
SuperStars

Personal file

Born: In Cork, Ireland, on August 10th, 1971
Height: 5ft 10in
Weight: 12st 10lb
Family: My Dad is Mossie, and my mum is Marie
Other Clubs: Nottingham Forest
Honours: ZDS Trophy 1992; Charity Shield 1993, 1996, 1997; FA Premiership 1994, 1996, 1997, 1999; FA Cup 1994, 1996, 1999; European Cup 1999; Rep of Ire Schools, Youth, U-21, full caps

When I was A boy

WHO WAS YOUR CHILDHOOD HERO?
The boxer Mike Tyson.

DID YOU PLAY ANY OTHER SPORTS?
I used to box, I had four fights and won them all. I also played a bit of Gaelic football and hurling. Real Irish sports.

WHAT WAS YOUR FIRST TEAM?
I used to play for a club called Rockmount back in Cork. I played for them for about seven or eight years and then I went to Cobh Ramblers for £40 a week.

WHAT WERE YOU LIKE AT SCHOOL?
It was just a distraction from football for me, I didn't really enjoy it. I just wanted to be outside, playing or training. Luckily enough it worked out - I don't know what I'd have done otherwise.

My Favourite...

MEAL: When I am not in training and can afford to relax a bit I do like a nice curry.
DRINK: When I'm in training it's normally isotonic drinks or just plain water to keep the fluids going into the body.
OTHER SPORTS: I'm a big boxing fan.
HOLIDAY DESTINATION: I like to get back to Cork as often as I can, I love it there with my family and my oldest friends.
OTHER CLUB: I always keep an eye out for Nottingham Forest's results because I spent several happy years there.

Talking Football

WHICH PLAYER DO YOU MOST ADMIRE?
Bryan Robson was an excellent central midfielder who I used to watch a lot when I was younger.

WHO ALWAYS GIVES YOU A TOUGH TIME?
Before I joined United I used to have a very tough time coming up against people like Gary Pallister and Steve Bruce. But I don't worry about my opponents too much.

WHO HAS BEEN THE BEST MANAGER YOU'VE WORKED UNDER?
I've only really played under two as a professional - and they've both been brilliant. Brian Clough was pretty unconventional, but we got on well, and I have nothing but respect for Alex Ferguson. He is without doubt the most important person at the club.

WHAT'S BEEN YOUR BIGGEST FOOTBALL THRILL?
United's first 'double' in 1994 and representing Ireland for the first time were both pretty special moments.

AND YOUR BIGGEST DISAPPOINTMENT?
The injury to my knee which kept me out of action for nearly all of the 1997-98 season was a nightmare. It's made me a bit of a different person - on and off the pitch.

Roy Keane

MANCHESTER UNITED & REPUBLIC OF IRELAND

Roy Keane
SuperStars

Personal file

Born: In Newcastle, on August 13th, 1970
Height: 6ft
Weight: 12st 6lb
Family: Dad Alan and Mum Anne. I also have an older sister called Karen.
Car: A Jaguar
Other Clubs: Southampton, Blackburn
Honours: FA Premiership 1995; England Youth, Under-21, 'B' and full caps

When I was A boy

WHO DID YOU SUPPORT AS A LAD?
My local team, Newcastle United.

WHAT WAS YOUR FIRST KIT?
It would have been a Newcastle one.

WHO WAS YOUR CHILDHOOD HERO?
Kevin Keegan, who went on to be my manager at Newcastle and England of course. I used to watch him from the terraces and admire his non-stop effort and will-to-win. I was really upset when he left the club as a player.

WHAT WERE YOU LIKE AT SCHOOL?
I was only really interested in being a footballer - I kicked a ball around all day at school, and all the time when I got home too.

My Favourite...

MEAL: Chicken, beans and pasta, which I like to wash down with a big glass of orange juice. Perfect.
FILM: I really enjoyed 'Another 48 Hours', with the American comedian Eddie Murphy.
OTHER SPORTSPERSON: I admire the golfer Nick Faldo for the way he holds his nerve in high-pressure situations.
MUSICIAN: Phil Collins.
ALBUM: Serious Hits Live.
ACTRESS: Patsy Kensit, who is now married to Liam Gallagher from Oasis.
HOLIDAY DESTINATION: The Algarve in Portugal.
GROUND: St. James' Park - Newcastle's ground. Our fans are simply the best in the world and they really deserve to see some success. They have had to wait a long time for a trophy, that's for sure.

Talking Football

WHICH PLAYER DO YOU MOST ADMIRE?
It's a close run thing between Gary Lineker and Pele. Gary is a great role model for youngsters, while Pele was the best ever.

WHO ALWAYS GIVES YOU A TOUGH TIME?
Arsenal's Tony Adams. He is very tough and brave.

WHO HAS BEEN THE BIGGEST INFLUENCE ON YOUR CAREER?
My parents. They gave up so much time to watch me play and drive me about - especially when I moved down south to play for Southampton in my teens.

WHAT'S BEEN YOUR BIGGEST FOOTBALL THRILL?
Scoring a goal on my England debut against France at Wembley was a memorable experience, as was winning the League with Blackburn in 1995. Also leading my country out is always magical. There is no higher honour in the game than being captain of your country. I'm just sad that my Grandfather didn't live to see me play for England. He'd have been so proud.

NEWCASTLE UNIT

SuperStars
Alan Shearer

LIVERPO
OTBALL C

Personal file

Born: In Ilford on October 27th, 1967
Height: 5ft 11in
Weight: 12st 2lb
Family: I was brought up by my aunt in London. I am married now, to Claire, and we have two sons
Honours: FA Cup 1990, 1994 ; Euro Cup-Winners' Cup 1991; European Super Cup 1991; League Cup 1992; FA Premiership 1993, 1994; Charity Shield 1993, 1994; England Youth, Under-21, 'B' and full caps

When I was A boy

WHO DID YOU SUPPORT AS A LAD?
Manchester United - or whoever was at the top of the First Division at the time! Like a lot of young kids, I changed my team almost every season.

WHAT WAS THE HIGHLIGHT OF YOUR SCHOOLDAYS?
Playing at Wembley in the Smith's Crisps Cup Final in 1979, when I was 12. That was my first trip to the national stadium and it made me want to become a professional.

WHO WAS YOUR CHILDHOOD HERO?
The former Man United winger Gordon Hill - he was brilliant.

WHAT WERE YOU LIKE AT SCHOOL?
I didn't learn much at school - I always wanted to be a footballer. Without football I don't know what I'd be doing with my life.

My Favourite...

MEAL: Chicken, pasta and beans.
FILM: I like action thrillers.
OTHER SPORTSPERSON: My cousin Nigel Benn, the former champion middleweight boxer. I'm also a big fan of Stephen Hendry, the World Snooker Champion.
BEST MATE IN FOOTBALL: I'm big pals with Ian Wright.
ACTRESS: Demi Moore.
HOLIDAY DESTINATION: Anywhere that I can relax and get away from football for a few weeks. America is good for that.

Talking Football

ARE YOU VERY SUPERSTITIOUS?
Yes, I think most footballers are. My main habit is that I only put my shirt on in the players' tunnel, just before I run out onto the pitch.

WHAT'S THE WORST ADVICE YOU'VE EVER BEEN GIVEN?
A guy called Eddie Bailey, who was a scout at West Ham when I was there as a youngster, once told me that I couldn't run, couldn't pass and would never make a footballer.

WHAT'S BEEN YOUR BEST FOOTBALL MOMENT?
I've been lucky enough to have many special moments, like captaining England and winning lots of trophies with Man United. Also, qualifying for the 1998 World Cup by drawing with Italy in Rome was a great night.

DO YOU LIKE BEING KNOWN AS A TOUGH TACKLER?
It can get on your nerves a bit. Personally, I think I've got a lot more to my game than just tackling hard.

WHAT ELSE DO YOU WANT TO ACHIEVE?
I'd dearly love to win the Championship with Liverpool, and also to help England qualify for Euro 2000. We've got a good side and under Kevin Keegan who knows what we can achieve.

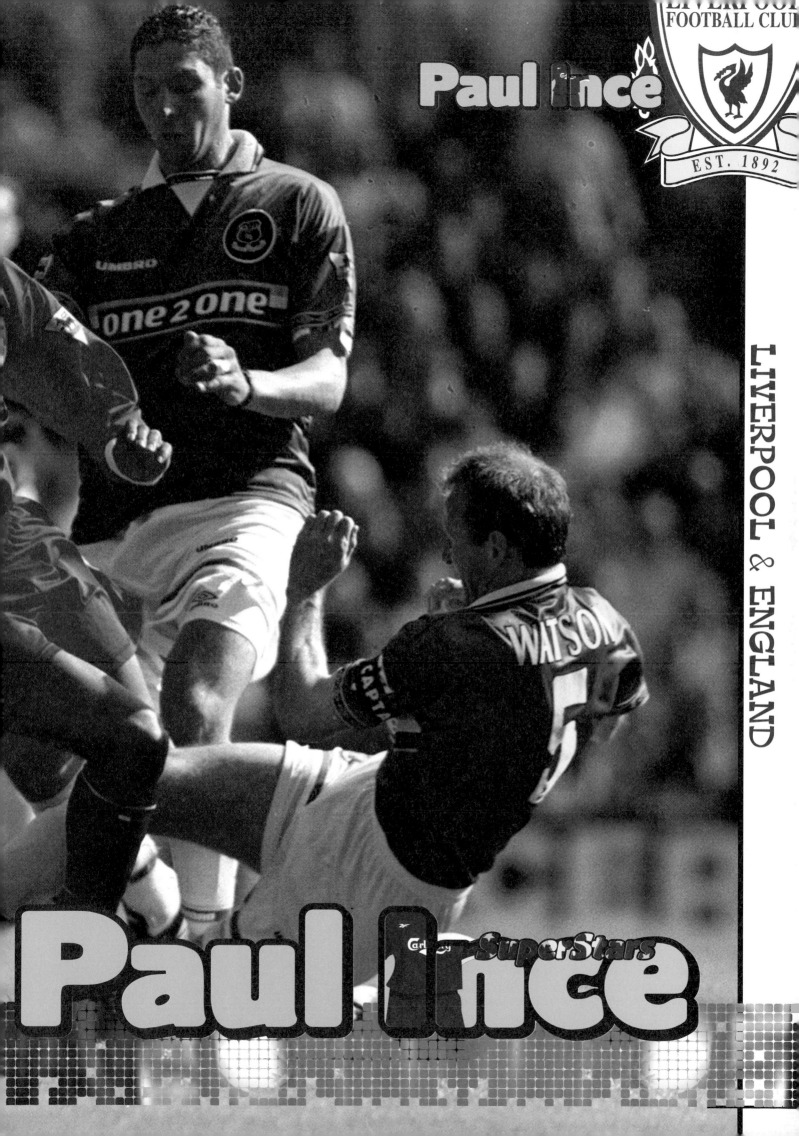

Paul Ince

LIVERPOOL
FOOTBALL CLUB
EST. 1892

LIVERPOOL & ENGLAND

Paul Ince

Personal file

Born: In Galashiels, on January 30th, 1968
Height: 5ft 7in
Weight: 10st 12lb
Family: I'm married to Susan and we have two daughters, six-year-old Hannah and Julia, four
Home: A lovely detached house on the Wirral
Car: Mercedes 320 CLK
Honours: Scottish Cup 1995; French League 1997; Scotland Youth, Under-21 and full caps

When I was A boy

WHO DID YOU SUPPORT AS A LAD?
Celtic. I remember getting their kit for Christmas when I was six.

WHO WAS YOUR CHILDHOOD HERO?
Maradona. He had fantastic skill and was also a great team player. I loved watching him take free-kicks - it inspired me.

WHAT WERE YOU LIKE AT SCHOOL?
Not too bad. I enjoyed Technical Drawing but I hated maths and chemistry. I just didn't understand them.

DID YOU STAY UP LATE TO WATCH MATCH OF THE DAY ON SATURDAY NIGHTS?
I certainly did, although it's called 'Sportscene' up in Scotland. Celtic were on it a lot, so I was always allowed to sit up late.

My Favourite...

MEAL: Chicken with sun-dried tomatoes and rice.
TV PROGRAMME: I don't really watch much TV, except if I'm sat down with the kids.
OTHER SPORTSPERSON: The basketball player Michael Jordan, a true superstar.
COMMENTATOR: I like John Motson.
ALBUM: I prefer compilation albums, but most of the music I hear these days comes from my girls' CD collections!
ACTOR/ACTRESS: I admire Anthony Hopkins and Michelle Pfeiffer.

Talking Football

WHICH OTHER PLAYER DO YOU MOST ADMIRE?
Zinedine Zidane, the French star. Not just because he's a midfielder like me, but because he combines his great skill with a willingness to tackle back and work hard for his team.

WHAT'S THE BEST GOAL YOU'VE EVER SCORED?
My penalty for Scotland against Brazil in the opening game of the 1998 World Cup.

AND THE BEST YOU'VE SEEN?
Maradona's amazing dribble for Argentina against England in the 1986 World Cup.

WHAT'S THE BEST MATCH YOU'VE EVER SEEN?
Everton fans might not like me for this, but it has to be Liverpool's 4-3 win over Newcastle a few years ago. I was in France at the time, and watched it on TV, and I couldn't believe I was seeing such a thrilling game. It was the kind of football that made me want to play in the Premiership.

HOW ABOUT THE BEST YOU'VE PLAYED IN?
The World Cup match against Brazil was fantastic, and also the game when I scored my first goal for Celtic against Rangers back in 1991. We won 2-1 that day and it was a truly memorable occasion.

John Collins

NIL SATIS NISI

EVERTON & SCOTLAND

SuperStars

John Collins

Personal file

Born: In Leytonstone, on May 2nd, 1975
Height: 6ft
Weight: 11st 12lb
Family: Mum is Sandra, dad is Ted
Other Clubs: Preston North End (on loan)
Honours: FA Premiership 1996, 1997, 1999; FA Cup 1996,1999; Charity Shield 1996, 1997; European Cup 1999, England Youth, Under-21 and full caps; PFA Young Player of the Year 1997

When I was A boy

WHO DID YOU SUPPORT AS A LAD?
I have always supported Manchester United. To be playing for them is like a dream come true.

WHAT WAS YOUR FIRST KIT?
Guess! I had a United kit, and used to get loads of stick from the kids for wearing my United scarf to school.

WHO WAS YOUR CHILDHOOD HERO?
Bryan Robson. I first saw him play when I was eight and he made me want to be a midfielder.

WHAT WERE YOU LIKE AT SCHOOL?
I used to sit at the back and chat with my mates. I was a good athlete and set the school 400 metres record - it still stands today I think. I also quite enjoyed the cooking lessons.

My Favourite...

MEAL: I really enjoy Chinese food, although I usually eat stuff like pasta before a game.

OTHER SPORTSPERSON: I'm quite good mates with a guy called Ronnie O'Sullivan, who is an excellent snooker player.

MUSICIAN: I like soul music and am a big fan of people like George Michael, R. Kelly and Stevie Wonder. And the Spice Girls, obviously!

HOLIDAY DESTINATION: Anywhere where Victoria and I can get away from things and really relax. Ireland, where we were married in the summer, is lovely.

GROUND: I still get a real buzz from playing at Old Trafford, especially in European games.

FRIEND: I get on well with Gary Neville, he's definitely one of my closest friends at United and we talk all the time. He was the best man at my wedding.

Talking Football

TELL US ABOUT JOINING UNITED...
I cried when my mum told me United wanted to sign me - I was so overcome!

WHAT ADVICE WOULD YOU GIVE TO A SOCCERSTARS READER WANTING TO BE THE 'NEXT DAVID BECKHAM'?
Enjoy your football and practice hard. It is not worth getting too serious yet - just go out and enjoy playing and practising.

WHO'S BEEN YOUR BIGGEST INFLUENCE?
Lots of people have helped me, but I have to say a big thank you to Alex Ferguson. I'll always be grateful to him.

WHAT'S BEEN YOUR BIGGEST FOOTBALL THRILL?
I'm lucky to have already had many exciting times in football - playing for England, playing in a World Cup and in FA Cup Finals.

AND YOUR BIGGEST DISAPPOINTMENT?
The way my World Cup ended was a big disappointment.

David Beckham

MANCHESTER UNITED FOOTBALL CLUB

MANCHESTER UNITED & ENGLAND

SuperStars

David Beckham

What do you remember

THE ANSWERS TO THESE QUESTIONS CAN ALL BE FOUND IN OUR SUPERSTARS SECTION.

1. FOR WHICH TEAM DID MICHAEL OWEN'S DAD PLAY PROFESSIONAL FOOTBALL - LIVERPOOL, EVERTON OR TOTTENHAM?

2. PAUL LAMBERT WON THE CHAMPIONS' LEAGUE WITH WHICH GERMAN CLUB?

3. ALAN SHEARER'S HERO WHEN HE WAS A BOY WAS KEVIN KEEGAN. TRUE OR FALSE?

4. DAVID BECKHAM IS MARRIED TO WHICH OF THE SPICE GIRLS?

5. RYAN GIGGS IS A BIG FAN OF RUGBY LEAGUE OR CRICKET?

6. WHICH OTHER CLUB'S RESULTS DOES ROY KEANE ALWAYS LOOK OUT FOR?

SOCCER STARS
QUIZ Time No.2

Who am i?

IT'S EASY IF YOU CAN SEE THE PICTURES BUT CAN YOU IDENTIFY THESE TWO MYSTERY PLAYERS?

1 I am the Ginger Spice at Old Trafford.
I play for England.
I scored in the World Cup against Tunisia.
I missed the Champions' League Final last year.
I can play in midfield or attack.

2 I play for a club in London.
I arrived in England from an Italian side.
I was voted Player of the Year in 1998.
I play for a country who wear orange shirts.
I wear the No.10 shirt.
I do not like flying in aeroplanes.

FIVE CHANGES HAVE BEEN MADE TO PICTURE B. CAN YOU SPOT THEM?

SPOT THE DiFFEReNCE

A

B

SOCCER STARS

Colour 'em in

DATAFILE

Name: Seamus John Given
Born: April 20th, 1976, in Lifford, Ireland
Height: 6ft 1in
Weight: 13st 4lb
Position: Goalkeeper
Other Clubs played for: Blackburn, Swindon (on loan), Sunderland (on loan)
Honours: First Division title 1996; Rep of Ireland Youth, Under-21 and full caps

SOCCER STARS — KEEPER RATING

HANDLING	4
SHOT STOPPING	5
THROWING	3
EXPERIENCE	4
KICKING	3

SOCCER STARS RATING ★★★★

ONE OF THE PREMIERSHIP'S BRIGHTEST YOUNG STOPPERS, HE HAS ALSO MADE THE IRELAND SHIRT HIS OWN SINCE HITTING THE BIG TIME IN 1995-96.

Jeepers Keepers

● Only a last minute change of position allowed Shay to go all the way to the top. All through his life he had played centre-forward - but as a teenager he had a go in goal and soon came to the attention of Celtic boss Liam Brady.

● Shay missed a chunk of Newcastle's 1997-98 campaign after getting injured while away on international duty with the Republic of Ireland.

● His international debut came against Russia in Dublin on 27th March 1996. Ireland lost the game 2-0 in what was Mick McCarthy's first game in charge. Shay hadn't even played a first-team game for Blackburn at that stage!

● On a happier note, Shay also played his part in the Republic's record away score, when they beat Liechtenstein 5-0 in a World Cup qualifier in August 1996.

● He picked up a First Division Championship medal while on loan with Sunderland in 1995-96. He kept 12 clean-sheets in 17 games for the club and they were keen to buy him at the end of the campaign, but Blackburn wouldn't let Given go.

Background Info

SHAY BEGAN HIS CAREER IN SCOTLAND WITH CELTIC, BUT FAILED TO MAKE THE GRADE AND WAS RELEASED TO BLACKBURN BEFORE SIGNING PRO. FRUSTRATED AT BEING UNDERSTUDY TO TIM FLOWERS AT EWOOD PARK HE REJOINED HIS FORMER MANAGER KENNY DALGLISH AT NEWCASTLE IN A £1.5M MOVE IN JULY 1997 AND QUICKLY ESTABLISHED HIMSELF AT ST. JAMES' PARK.

SHAY SAYS

"I WAS PLAYING FOR IRELAND BUT I COULDN'T GET INTO THE BLACKBURN TEAM, TIM FLOWERS WAS ALWAYS THE FIRST CHOICE. I HEARD THAT KENNY DALGLISH WAS INTERESTED IN TAKING ME TO NEWCASTLE AND I WAS ABSOLUTELY DELIGHTED TO MAKE THE MOVE WHEN THE CHANCE AROSE."

"THE NOISE FROM THE NEWCASTLE FANS IS AMAZING - SOMETIMES THEY DON'T STOP SINGING ALL GAME. THERE'S SUCH A BUZZ DURING THE BIG MATCHES, YOU CAN TELL HOW IMPORTANT THE GAME IS FROM THE CROWD NOISE."

"IT IS AN AMAZING HONOUR TO PLAY FOR YOUR COUNTRY AT ANY LEVEL, BUT ESPECIALLY IN THE SENIOR SIDE. I'M VERY PROUD TO WEAR THE JERSEY."

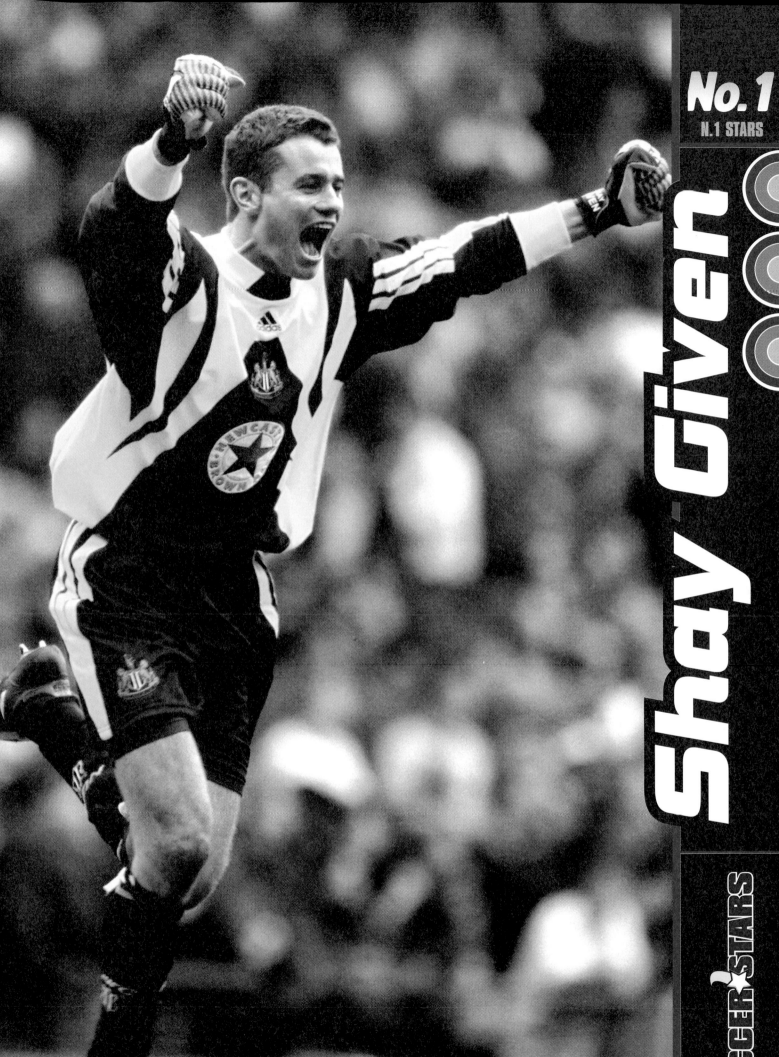

No. 1

N.1 STARS

Shay Given

SOCCER STARS

DATAFILE

Name: Neil Hislop
Born: February 22nd, 1969, in Hackney
Height: 6ft 4in
Weight: 14st 4lb
Position: Goalkeeper
Other clubs played for: Reading, Newcastle
Nickname: Shaka
Honours: Second Division title 1994; England Under-21 and 'B' caps

SOCCER STARS

KEEPER RATING		
HANDLING	VVVV	4
SHOT STOPPING	VVVV	4
THROWING	VVVV	4
EXPERIENCE	VVV	3
KICKING	VVVV	4

SOCCER STARS RATING
★★★★

A GIANT 'KEEPER WITH GREAT REFLEXES, SHAKA HAS PUT A COUPLE OF POOR YEARS BEHIND HIM TO RE-ESTABLISH HIMSELF AT THE TOP LEVEL WITH WEST HAM.

Jeepers Keepers

● Shaka admits that he is still disappointed at failing to reach the top flight with Reading a few years back. The Royals lost 4-3 in the Play-Off Final against Bolton, after leading 2-0. "It would have been such a massive achievement for a club like Reading to reach the Premiership. It still upsets me that we missed out," he says.

● An England Under-21 international, Shaka was called up to the 'B' and full squads during the 1997-98 campaign - but failed to figure in the senior side.

● A keen cricket fan - and a big mate of West Indies skipper Brian Lara - Shaka is actually a pretty mean fast bowler himself.

● At 6ft 4in, Shaka is one of the tallest players in the League - but even he is dwarfed by Oxford striker Kevin Francis, who measures up at a whopping 6ft 7in!

● When West Ham play Man Utd there is a little extra incentive for Shaka to stop The Red Devils scoring. He is close friends with United striker Dwight Yorke and the pair of them always have a bet on who is going to come out on top when they clash.

Background Info

SPOTTED PLAYING FOR HOWARD UNIVERSITY IN AMERICA, SHAKA WAS SNAPPED UP BY READING IN SEPTEMBER 1992 AND WON MANY FANS AS HE HELPED THE ROYALS TO THE SECOND DIVISION TITLE IN 1994. IT CAME AS LITTLE SURPRISE WHEN HE STEPPED UP TO THE TOP FLIGHT, JOINING NEWCASTLE FOR £1.575 MILLION IN AUGUST 1995. WEST HAM SIGNED HIM ON A FREE TRANSFER IN THE SUMMER OF 1998.

SHAKA SAYS

"I'VE ALREADY PLAYED FOR THE ENGLAND 'B' TEAM, AND I WAS ON THE BENCH FOR THE MATCH AGAINST CHILE A COUPLE OF SEASONS BACK, AND THAT HAS MADE ME HUNGRY FOR MORE. I HOPE I GET ANOTHER CALL - THERE AREN'T TOO MANY GOOD ENGLISH 'KEEPERS ABOUT, SO I'VE GOT TO BE OPTIMISTIC ABOUT MY CHANCES."

"I HAVE TO GIVE HARRY REDKNAPP A LOT OF THANKS FOR SHOWING FAITH IN ME. HE BROUGHT ME IN FROM NEWCASTLE AND GAVE ME THE CHANCE TO PLAY FIRST-TEAM FOOTBALL AGAIN AT WEST HAM."

"THERE ARE SIX BASIC RULES TO REMEMBER IF YOU WANT TO BE A TOP 'KEEPER: DEDICATION, DON'T LOSE HEART, BE BRAVE, LOOK AFTER YOURSELF, TRAIN HARD AND LISTEN TO ADVICE. IF YOU WORK AT ALL OF THOSE YOU WILL BE IN WITH A CHANCE."

Shaka Hislop

SOCCER★STARS

Neil Sullivan

Neil Sullivan

SOCCER STARS

KEEPER RATING

HANDLING	☝☝☝☝	4
SHOT STOPPING	☝☝☝☝	4
THROWING	☝☝☝☝☝	5
EXPERIENCE	☝☝☝	3
KICKING	☝☝☝☝☝	5

SOCCER STARS RATING
★★★★

NEIL HAS ESTABLISHED HIMSELF AS ONE OF THE PREMIERSHIP'S TOP STOPPERS OVER THE LAST COUPLE OF SEASONS AND IS NOW SCOTLAND'S FIRST CHOICE NO.1.

DATAFILE

Name: Neil Sullivan
Born: February 24th, 1970, in Sutton
Height: 6ft
Weight: 12st 1lb
Position: Goalkeeper
Other Clubs played for: Crystal Palace (on loan)
Nickname: Sully
Honours: Scotland full caps

Jeepers Keepers

● Neil's most disappointing season yet came in 1996-97, when The Dons were chasing the 'treble' of League, FA Cup and League Cup but ended empty-handed. They reached the Semi-Final of the two Cup competitions and slipped to eighth place in the Premiership - so missed out on Europe too!

● Having kept three successive clean-sheets, Neil suffered a broken leg in a match against Nott'm Forest at the end of the 1994-95 season.

● Sully was the victim of that David Beckham goal when Becks chipped him from 50 yards at the start of the 1996-97 season. In the following match David Batty left Neil sick again when he lobbed the ball over him from 30 yards!

● Neil's international debut for Scotland came against Wales at Rugby Park, Kilmarnock, in May 1997. It wasn't the best of starts, as Scotland lost the match 1-0.

● While many footballers drive fast, flash motors, Neil is a fan of vintage cars and has a small collection of old vehicles of which he is very proud.

Background Info

A TRIUMPH FOR WIMBLEDON'S SCOUTING SYSTEM, NEIL CAME UP THROUGH THE RANKS AT SELHURST PARK, SPENDING SEVERAL YEARS AS SECOND IN LINE BEHIND HANS SEGERS FOR THE GOALKEEPER'S SPOT. HE FIRST BROKE INTO THE SIDE IN 1990-91, BUT IT WASN'T UNTIL THE 1996-97 SEASON THAT HE REALLY ESTABLISHED HIMSELF.

SULLY SAYS

"THEY'VE ALWAYS HAD A CRAZY BUNCH OF LADS AT THIS CLUB - IT'S PART OF WHAT MAKES WIMBLEDON SUCH A SPECIAL TEAM. WHEN I WAS IN THE YOUTH TEAM WE'D GET BEATEN UP ONCE A WEEK BY THE FIRST-TEAM...I DON'T KNOW WHAT IT'S LIKE AT OTHER CLUBS, WHETHER IT'S NORMAL OR NOT!"

"I'VE BEEN HERE 15 YEARS, SO IT WOULD BE A BIG WRENCH TO LEAVE. YOU NEVER KNOW WHAT IS AROUND THE CORNER, BUT I HAVE NO INTENTION OF MOVING ON. I'M HAPPY HERE."

"THE LADS ALL TOOK THE MICKEY OUT OF ME A BIT, AS I WAS BORN IN SURREY AND HAVE A LONDON ACCENT, BUT I'M PROUD TO PLAY FOR SCOTLAND. LOTS OF MY FAMILY COME FROM THE COUNTRY."

Nigel Martyn

SOCCER STARS

SOCCER STARS

HANDLING	⟨⟨⟨⟨	4
SHOT STOPPING	⟨⟨⟨⟨⟨	5
THROWING	⟨⟨⟨⟨	4
EXPERIENCE	⟨⟨⟨⟨	4
KICKING	⟨⟨⟨⟨	4

SOCCER STARS RATING
★★★★★

ONE OF THE SAFEST 'KEEPERS AROUND, LEEDS MAN NIGEL IS THE NEXT IN LINE FOR THE ENGLAND JOB ONCE ARSENAL'S DAVID SEAMAN CALLS IT A DAY.

KEEPER RATING

Nigel Martyn

DATAFILE

Name: Anthony Nigel Martyn
Born: August 11th, 1966, in St. Austell
Height: 6ft 2in
Weight: 14st 7lb
Position: Goalkeeper
Other Clubs played for: Bristol Rovers, Crystal Palace
Honours: Third Division title 1990; ZDS Trophy 1991; First Division title 1994; England Under-21, 'B' and full caps

Jeepers Keepers

● Nigel was once memorably described as 'The Cornishman with the frying pan hands' by BBC Radio Five Live commentator Stuart Hall. You what?!

● As a boy he used to play on the wing, but went in goal when his side's regular 'keeper failed to turn up for a game - and he has stayed there ever since.

● Martyn was part of Crystal Palace's most successful ever side. Along with fellow England internationals Ian Wright, Andy Gray, Geoff Thomas and John Salako, the goalkeeper inspired The Eagles to a third place finish in the top flight back in 1991.

● His England debut came during a 2-2 draw with the CIS on 29th April 1992, when he appeared as a substitute for Sheffield Wednesday's Chris Woods. CIS stood for 'Commonwealth of Independent States', and was a team formed after the collapse of the Soviet Union in 1991.

● Nigel enjoys days out with his family at theme parks and isn't afraid to test his nerves on the big wheel or rollercoaster!

Background Info

BRITAIN'S FIRST £1 MILLION GOALKEEPER, NIGEL WAS DISCOVERED PLAYING NON-LEAGUE FOOTBALL WITH VILLAGE SIDE ST. BLAZEY IN CORNWALL. HE SIGNED FOR BRISTOL ROVERS IN AUGUST 1987 AND WON ENGLAND UNDER-21 CAPS BEFORE TRANSFERRING TO C. PALACE IN THAT RECORD-BREAKING MOVE IN NOVEMBER 1989. HE JOINED LEEDS FOR £2.25 MILLION IN JULY 1996.

NIGEL SAYS

"THERE AREN'T TOO MANY BAD STRIKERS IN THE PREMIERSHIP, BUT ALAN SHEARER AND PAUL SCHOLES REALLY STICK OUT IN TERMS OF FINISHING. THEY ARE BOTH TOP NOTCH."

"SINCE I FIRST BROKE INTO THE ENGLAND SQUAD I HAVE ALWAYS BEEN INVOLVED IN THE 22. YOU CAN'T TAKE ANYTHING FOR GRANTED, BUT I SEEM TO HAVE A REGULAR PLACE. NOW I'VE JUST GOT TO GET RID OF DAVID SEAMAN!"

"I SIGNED A NEW CONTRACT LAST SEASON BECAUSE I WANT TO WIN THINGS AND I BELIEVE I CAN DO THAT WITH LEEDS. THE MANAGER, DAVID O'LEARY, HAS NOT BEEN IN THE POSITION LONG, BUT I THINK HE'S PROVED WHAT A GOOD JOB HE CAN DO."

What do you remember

THE ANSWERS TO THESE QUESTIONS CAN ALL BE FOUND IN OUR NO.1 STARS SECTION.

1. SHAY GIVEN PLAYS FOR WALES, NORTHERN IRELAND OR THE REPUBLIC OF IRELAND?

2. NIGEL MARTYN IS THE FIRST CHOICE 'KEEPER AT WHICH CLUB?

3. SHAKA HISLOP IS BIG MATES WITH WHICH MAN UNITED STAR?

4. NEIL SULLIVAN IS PART OF WHICH GANG AT WIMBLEDON?

5. WHICH OF THE FAB FOUR 'KEEPERS LEFT CRYSTAL PALACE TO HEAD TO ELLAND ROAD?

6. WHO GREW UP ON THE ISLAND OF TOBAGO?

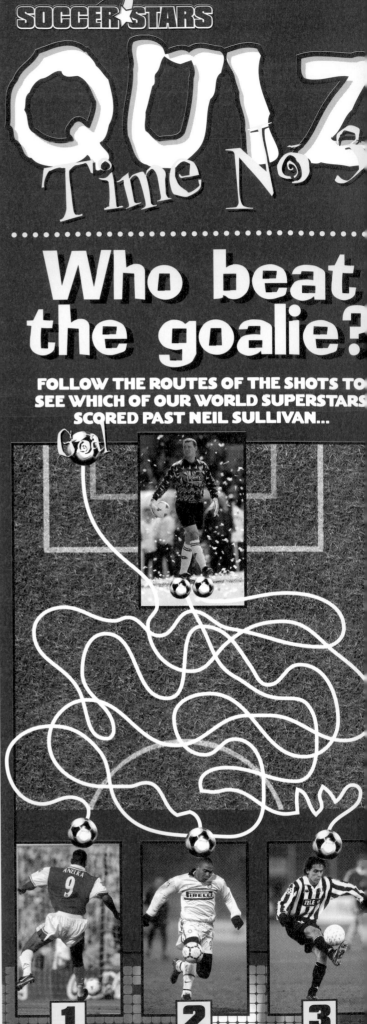

SOCCER STARS
QUIZ Time No3

Who beat the goalie?

FOLLOW THE ROUTES OF THE SHOTS TO SEE WHICH OF OUR WORLD SUPERSTARS SCORED PAST NEIL SULLIVAN...

Goal

1 **2** **3**

IDENTITY PARADE

OUR PHOTOGRAPHER HAD THE WOBBLES TAKING PICTURES OF
THESE NINE STAR PLAYERS. DO YOU KNOW WHO THEY ARE?

1

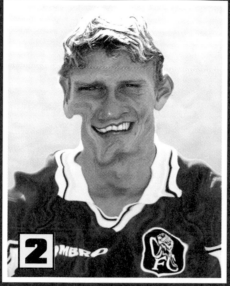

2

3

5

6

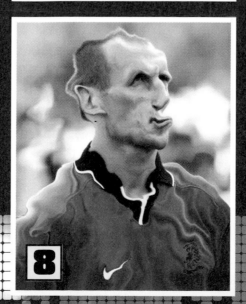

8

9

Kieron Dyer Ipswich

All about Kieron

WHAT'S HIS BACKGROUND?

Born in Ipswich, Kieron played in the same youth football side as his Ipswich and England team-mate Richard Wright and Arsenal's Matt Upson. He soon came to the attention of the Ipswich Town scouts and has been with the club since he was 11. He made his debut as an 18-year-old and has never looked back.

SO WAS HE AN IPSWICH FAN AS A KID?

Not really no. Despite living a couple of hundred miles away he followed Liverpool in his early days. His hero was the midfielder John Barnes, who young Kieron always used to pretend to be when he was kicking about in the park.

DATAFILE

Name: Kieron Courtney Dyer
Born: December 29th, 1978 in Ipswich
Height: 5ft 7in
Weight: 9st 7lbs
Position: Midfield or wing-back
Clubs played for: Ipswich
Nickname: Special K

HE LOOKS A BIT SMALL TO BE A FOOTBALLER, HOW DOES HE COPE?

Kieron's not the biggest lad in the world, and some opponents do try to kick him out of the game - but he's pretty tough. He broke his leg against Watford last season, but generally he uses his pace and fitness to keep himself out of harm's way.

WHAT DOES HE LIKE TO DO WHEN HE'S NOT PLAYING?

He's a very keen pool player and also loves mixing tunes on his decks - he often rings pals up and plays them his new sounds down the phone! He's a big fan of cars, too, and last season bought himself a flash black top of the range Porsche Boxter.

They say

Rising Star

"Kieron is one of the best young midfielders in the country - right up there with people like Frank Lampard and Lee Hendrie."
Man United and England Under-21 star JOHN CURTIS

Who does he play like?

Fans at Portman Road reckon Kieron's like a cross between Gazza and Leeds' Lee Bowyer. He combines tons of clever skills and tricks with great pace and stamina allowing him to cover an awful lot of ground during a match.

Where next?

The first two seasons of Kieron's career saw him go from Ipswich unknown to the full England squad - from here, the sky is the limit for this gifted youngster.

SOCCER STARS

SKILL	4
HEADING	3
PASSING	4
SHOOTING	3
SPEED	4
TACKLING	3
TEMPER	4

SOCCER STARS RATING
★ ★ ★ ★

SKILL CHART

Rising Star

DATAFILE

Name: Rio Gavin Ferdinand
Born: November 7th, 1978 in Peckham
Height: 6ft 2in
Weight: 12st 1lb
Position: Defender
Clubs played for: West Ham, Bournemouth (on loan)
Nickname(s): Ferdy, Class

They say

"Rio is my best mate and he is pretty faultless as a player. He can play in almost any position, he is quick, skilful and good in the air - class all round really."
West Ham team-mate FRANK LAMPARD

Who does he play like?

Rio's similar to Frank Leboeuf. His skill and awareness make him a natural at bringing the ball out of defence and he is comfortable attacking as well. Old-timers compare him to Bobby Moore - the Hammers captain who won the 1966 World Cup with England.

Where next?

Cool, calm and classy on the ball, Rio made his international debut as a teenager and looks set to be an automatic choice in England's defence for many, many years to come. Could even be a future skipper of club and country.

All about Rio

RIO MUST HAVE BEEN PLAYING FOOTBALL SINCE HE WAS A NIPPER, HASN'T HE?

Yes and no. He kicked a ball around like most young lads, but was more interested in other sports like basketball and gymnastics. He didn't take up football seriously until he was 12, when he joined West Ham's School of Excellence.

BUT AFTER THAT IT'S BEEN SUCCESS ALL THE WAY, RIGHT?

Pretty much. He was converted from striker to defender during his first year at Upton Park and signed pro forms in November 1995, just after his 17th birthday. Six months later he led The Hammers to the FA Youth Cup Final and the South East Counties League Championship.

HE'S BEEN INVOLVED WITH ENGLAND FOR QUITE A TIME TOO, HASN'T HE?

He picked up Youth caps as a striker and also played for the Under-21s. But in May 1996 he was called up to train with the full England squad ahead of Euro 96 - while still only 17. He's now a regular in the senior side.

IS THERE ANYTHING ELSE WE SHOULD KNOW ABOUT HIM?

Well, his cousin is Les Ferdinand, the Tottenham and England striker. The two only met when Les was at QPR and Rio attended a training session with the Loftus Road club!

SOCCER STARS

SKILL	4
HEADING	4
PASSING	4
SHOOTING	3
SPEED	4
TACKLING	4
TEMPER	4

SOCCER STARS RATING ★★★★★

SKILL CHART

Rio Ferdinand West Ham

LIVERPOOL FOOTBALL CLUB

DATAFILE

Name: James Lee Carragher
Born: January 28th, 1978 in Bootle
Height: 6ft
Weight: 12st
Position: Central Defender
Clubs played for: Liverpool
Nickname(s): J, Carro

Rising Star

They say

"I reckon Jamie has got a massive future in front of him. He is one of the best defenders we have had in years and I am confident he will go on to play regularly for England."

JAMIE REDKNAPP

Who does he play like?

Despite beginning life as a midfielder, Jamie has turned into a real talent in defence. A tough tackler who can play the ball out from the back with confidence, Liverpool fans think they have unearthed their very own Sol Campbell in Jamie.

Where next?

He could save Liverpool £10m by becoming the answer to their central defensive problems. Already an England Under-21 and 'B' international, it can only be a matter of time before Jamie starts challenging the likes of Tottenham's Sol Campbell and Rio Ferdinand, of West Ham, for their places in the senior squad.

All about Jamie

SO WHERE'S HE ARRIVED FROM THEN?

One of the few Liverpool-born stars in the current Reds side, Jamie has been with the club since he was a youngster, coming up through the ranks at Anfield to become a first-team regular. He played in midfield in the same team as Michael Owen as Liverpool won the FA Youth Cup in 1996, beating West Ham in the Final.

HANG ON, YOU SAID HE WAS A DEFENDER - HOW COME HE WAS PLAYING IN MIDFIELD IN THOSE DAYS?

He used to be a midfielder, but was pushed back into defence by coach Phil Thompson, who reckons Jamie's a world-beater. "I don't care where I play, so long as I get a game," says Jamie. "I used to think midfield was my best position, but now I'm a defender. I can adapt to both."

LIVERPOOL AREN'T AT THEIR BEST IN CENTRAL DEFENCE, ARE THEY?

A whole string of players have tried their luck in that position for the Reds in recent years - Neil Ruddock, John Scales, Phil Babb, Rigobert Song - but local hero Jamie is probably the best of the lot.

WHAT'S BEEN THE HIGHLIGHT OF HIS CAREER SO FAR?

Well he's won caps at every level including full international for England, but the player himself reckons it was his full debut for Liverpool. "Playing against Aston Villa and scoring was a great moment for me," recalls Jamie.

SOCCER STARS

Skill	Rating
SKILL	4
HEADING	4
PASSING	4
SHOOTING	3
SPEED	3
TACKLING	4
TEMPER	4

SOCCER STARS **RATING** ★★★★

SKILL CHART

YOU'LL NEVER WALK ALONE

LIVERPOOL
FOOTBALL CLUB

EST. 1892

Jamie Carragher Liverpool

LEEDS UNITED AFC

Alan Smith Leeds

All about Alan

SO WHAT'S HIS BACKGROUND?

Well, he attended the FA School of Excellence along with Everton's Francis Jeffers but left when he was 15 because he was homesick. The school takes the elite young players and grooms them for professional soccer but Alan got homesick and left early.

DID THAT HARM HIS CHANCES OF MAKING IT BIG?

Not really. He was confident that he had the talent to play for the club he supported most of his life, Leeds - and he did.

HE MADE AN IMMEDIATE IMPACT, DIDN'T HE?

You could say that. He made his Leeds debut at Anfield last season and came off the bench to help his side to a 3-2 victory. Amazingly he scored with his first touch.

DID HE STAY IN THE TEAM?

Sure did. Alan is one of a crop of young stars coming up through the ranks at Leeds. Jonathan Woodgate and Steve McPhail are just two of the others and they, like Alan, are first team regulars now. With those three around, the future certainly looks bright at Elland Road.

DATAFILE

Name: Alan Smith
Born: October 28th, 1980 in Wakefield
Height: 5ft 9in
Weight: 10st 6lb
Position: Striker
Clubs played for: Leeds
Nickname: Smithy

They say

Rising Star

"Alan has a great future ahead of him. He has had a dream start playing for Leeds and now, if he keeps his head down and carries on learning, he could go on to achieve some wonderful things in this game."
Leeds boss DAVID O'LEARY

He is quick and strong and has a real eye for goal. Give him half a chance and he'll have a shot. Prefers to run at defenders than play as a target man and reminds many people of Man United's Ole Gunnar Solskjaer.

Who does he play like?

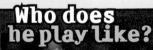

Where next?

Capped by England at Youth level, Alan seems certain to progress through the Under-21s to become a contender for a striker's role in the Full squad in time for the next World Cup in 2002.

SOCCER STARS

SKILL CHART

SKILL		4
HEADING		3
PASSING		3
SHOOTING		4
SPEED		4
TACKLING		4
TEMPER		4

SOCCER STARS RATING ★★★★

Francis Jeffers *Everton*

All about Francis

SO THE YOUNGSTER MUST BE PRETTY HIGHLY-RATED THEN?

He certainly is. So much so that ex-Everton boss Howard Kendall gave him his debut as a 16-year-old trainee on Boxing Day 1997 - away at Man United - making him the second youngest Everton player of all time. Two months later he signed a five-year contract reportedly worth a cool £1 million.

BUT DIDN'T THINGS GO A BIT DOWNHILL AFTER THAT BRILLIANT START?

They did - but not through any fault of his own. Just weeks after that dramatic debut, Francis woke up in the middle of the night with severe chest pains. It turned out to be a heart virus and kept him out of action for more than two months. "It ran through my head every day that it might be the end of my career," admits the youngster. Happily he is OK again now.

HE'S NOT THE ONLY EXCITING EVERTON YOUNGSTER EITHER, IS HE?

He's not, although he is the only one that was born within a throw-in of the ground and has supported the Goodison Park club all his life. But with other ace young players like Danny Cadamarteri, John Oster and Michael Ball in the squad, the future's looking a bit brighter for The Toffees.

DATAFILE

Name: Francis Jeffers
Born: January 25th, 1981 in Liverpool
Height: 5ft 10in
Weight: 10st 7lb
Position: Striker
Clubs played for: Everton
Nickname: Franny

They say

Rising Star

"Francis and Danny Cadamarteri did brilliantly for us last season. A year earlier they were up front when we won the FA Youth Cup and then in 1998-99 they were doing well in the Premiership - it shows how good the youngsters are at Everton."
Everton skipper **DAVE WATSON**

A quick, clever striker with an eye for goal, Jeffers is constantly compared to his Liverpool rival Michael Owen - who was a year above him at Lilleshall. Both have terrific pace, are stronger than they look and score loads of goals.

Who does he play like?

Where next?

With all Everton's scoring problems over the past few seasons it seems certain that Jeffers will become a regular up front for The Toffees soon rather than later. He is one of the brightest talents around.

SOCCER STARS

SKILL CHART

Skill	Rating
SKILL	4
HEADING	3
PASSING	3
SHOOTING	4
SPEED	4
TACKLING	3
TEMPER	4

SOCCER STARS RATING
★ ★ ★ ★

DATAFILE

Name: Wesley Michael Brown
Born: March 16th, 1979 in Manchester
Height: 6ft 1in
Weight: 12st 2lb
Position: Defender
Clubs played for: Manchester United
Nickname: Browny

Rising Star

They say

"Wes has got a massive future in front of him. I have seen a lot of quality young international players in my time and I think he will definitely be an England star."
United team-mate JAAP STAM

Who does he play like?

With his commanding presence at the back and skill bringing the ball forward, Wes is similar in style to former Man United defender, now Middlesbrough star, Gary Pallister, who helped his career develop at Old Trafford.

Where next?

Already a full England international and pushing hard for a place in United's first-team ahead of established stars like Ronny Johnsen and Henning Berg, Wes looks set for a glittering future with club and country.

All about Wes

WHAT CHANCE HAS WES GOT OF MAKING IT AT UNITED?

Every chance. United have one of the best records in the country for bringing on ace young players. Born in Manchester - and a Red Devils fan as a kid - Wes joins the likes of the Neville brothers, Paul Scholes, David Beckham and Ryan Giggs in stepping up from the impressive Old Trafford Youth team.

WHO HAVE BEEN HIS BIGGEST INFLUENCES AS A PLAYER?

Wes was lucky enough to be growing up at United at a time when Steve Bruce and Gary Pallister were just about the best central defensive partnership in the country. "Gary was a great help," remembers Wes. "He was always telling me what to do on the pitch and I learned a lot from both him and Steve."

HE SOUNDS A FAIRLY TASTY PLAYER, BUT WE HAVEN'T HEARD TOO MUCH ABOUT HIM. WHY IS THAT?

Like many United stars before him, Wes has been shielded by Alex Ferguson from a lot of the media spotlight, allowing him to concentrate everything on his football instead of doing interviews. "That's a good thing because I don't have that many distractions," explains Wes.

SO ARE WE LIKELY TO HEAR MORE FROM HIM IN THE FUTURE THEN?

Sure are. Happy playing at full-back or in the centre of defence, he burst onto the Premiership scene with United last season and has already made his debut for England.

SOCCER STARS

SKILL	3
HEADING	4
PASSING	3
SHOOTING	3
SPEED	4
TACKLING	4
TEMPER	4

SOCCER STARS RATING
★ ★ ★ ★

SKILL CHART

MANCHESTER UNITED FOOTBALL

Wes Brown Man United

Lee Hendrie Aston Villa

All about Lee

ISN'T HE THE GUY WHO HAD SUCH A BRILLIANT START TO LAST SEASON?

The very same. Just like his club, Aston Villa, Hendrie enjoyed an explosive start to the 1998-99 campaign - peaking with a call-up to the England side against the Czech Republic at Wembley, when he played a blinder.

PLAYING FOR ENGLAND? BUT SURELY HENDRIE IS A SCOTTISH NAME...

Well that's an interesting point. Lee's dad Paul (who played for Birmingham) and cousin John (ex-Barnsley) are both Scots, but Lee himself was born in Birmingham and opted to represent England when the chance arose. Not too sure how the family felt about that one!

D A T A F I L E

Name: Lee Andrew Hendrie
Born: May 18th, 1977 in Birmingham
Height: 5ft 10in
Weight: 10st 3lb
Position: Midfield
Clubs played for: Aston Villa
Nickname: Hendo

IT MUST BE TOUGH FOR A YOUNG PLAYER, HAVING FAMOUS RELATIVES TO LIVE UP TO...

It can increase the pressure a bit, but Lee insists that he was never pushed into being a footballer. "I've always played because I have wanted to," says Lee. "My dad's given me advice and stuff, but he's never forced me into things."

IT MUST HAVE BEEN A SURPRISE TO BE CALLED UP FOR ENGLAND...

"I was thrilled to bits and totally amazed," recalls Lee about his call-up. "I never thought I would make my England debut so early in my career. I was so nervous - I didn't think any of the other players would know who I was!"

They say

"Everyone is talking about the youngsters at Villa, and Lee Hendrie is one of the best. He has shown great maturity and I am confident that he can handle anything that is put before him."
Aston Villa and England star
PAUL MERSON

A hard-working and skilful midfielder like Man United's Paul Scholes, Lee loves to get forward to support his front men. But he can just as often be found scrapping it out in the midfield to help set-up chances for others.

Who does he play like?

Where next?

After such an explosive start things were bound to quieten down a bit for Lee last term. But on his best form he is among the country's most exciting midfielders and will be pushing for a regular international spot.

SOCCER STARS

SKILL	4
HEADING	3
PASSING	4
SHOOTING	4
SPEED	3
TACKLING	4
TEMPER	4

SKILL CHART

SOCCER STARS **RATING**
★★★★

What do you remember

THE ANSWERS TO THESE QUESTIONS CAN ALL BE FOUND IN OUR RISING STARS SECTION.

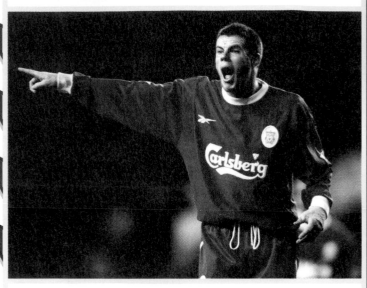

1. IN WHICH POSITION DOES IPSWICH'S KIERON DYER PLAY?

2. IS RIO FERDINAND A FULL ENGLAND INTERNATIONAL?

3. WES BROWN PLAYS FOR LIVERPOOL OR MANCHESTER UNITED?

4. FRANCIS JEFFERS MADE HIS DEBUT FOR EVERTON AT GOODISON PARK OR OLD TRAFFORD?

5. HAS LEE HENDRIE HAD ANY OTHER CLUBS APART FROM ASTON VILLA?

6. WHO IS ALAN SMITH'S MANAGER AT LEEDS UNITED?

SOCCER STARS

QUIZ Time No.4

Missing CLUBS

BELOW ARE FIVE PREMIERSHIP STARS WITH A LIST OF CLUBS THEY HAVE PLAYED FOR DURING THEIR CAREERS. CAN YOU FILL IN THE GAPS?

PAUL INCE   [ ]   MAN UNITED   INTER MILAN   LIVERPOOL

ALAN SHEARER   SOUTHAMPTON   [ ]   NEWCASTL

ANDY COLE   ARSENAL   BRISTOL CITY   [ ]   MAN UNIT

LES FERDINAND   [ ]   BESIKTAS   NEWCASTLE   TOTTENHA

IAN WRIGHT   C.PALACE   [ ]   WEST HA

You've been framed!

There are five things wrong with this picture. Can you find them?

SHOOTING

TIP FROM THE STARS

"Don't always look to hit the ball really hard. Sometimes you can place the ball past the 'keeper and score more easily than trying to break the net. It is also better to keep your shots low because it is harder for a 'keeper to make a save low down on the ground. And keep practising."
ALAN SHEARER

HOW DO YOU HIT THE BALL REALLY HARD?

Shooting is not all about power. It is about accuracy as well. No good hitting the ball at 100mph but miles wide, is it? To get a good connection, you need to have your non-kicking foot next to the ball and swing your other leg right back and then through to make contact. Carry on following through with your leg after you have hit the ball.

WHAT ARE THE MAIN THINGS TO DO?

Timing is the key. You can swing your leg as hard as you like, but if you are not balanced properly and don't make the right connection your shot will be pretty weak. Keep your head down as you make contact, too, otherwise the ball will just fly in the air and you won't look good.

HOW CAN YOU PRACTISE

You can practise striking the ball against a wall and then move further back as you get more confident. Also you can get a friend to go in goal and practise shooting from close in, moving back as you get better.

HEADING

DOESN'T IT HURT WHEN YOU HEAD THE BALL?

Not if you do it properly. If you use your forehead to head the ball, just above the eyes, you will be amazed how far you can head it - and it won't hurt either.

WHAT ARE THE KEY THINGS TO DO?

Keep your eyes on the ball at all times and try and make contact using your forehead, rather than the top of the head.

HOW CAN YOU PRACTISE?

You will need a friend to help you. Take it in turns to throw the ball to each other, heading the ball back to your partner. Practise heading the ball down to your friend's feet (like a striker heading at goal) and high up into the air (like a defender might at a corner). Also, have a go at jumping high in the air to make contact with the ball.

A COOL FOOTBALLER

CONTROL

TIP FROM THE STARS

"Football is very fast nowadays and you must have good control. I have always practised with the ball a great deal because that is the best way to improve your skills. Even throwing the ball in the air and controlling it will make you a better player."
GIANFRANCO ZOLA

WHY IS IT IMPORTANT?

Good control is essential. It allows you extra time to do what you want with the ball, like pass to a team-mate, make a cross into the penalty area or shoot at goal.

TIP FROM THE STARS

"Keep your eyes focused on the ball at all times and not on your opponent."
COLIN HENDRY

WHAT IS THE BEST WAY OF CONTROLLING THE BALL?

You can use your chest, thigh or toe to control the ball, depending on what height it comes at you. But mostly you will use the inside of your foot to receive a pass.

WHAT ARE THE MAIN THINGS TO DO?

Relaxing is the key. If you are tense, the ball will just bounce off you when it hits your body. You must get your foot, chest or thigh to act like a cushion and almost bend with the ball as it makes contact. If you do that, the ball will drop nicely to the floor for you to kick it where you want to.

HOW DO YOU PRACTISE?

If you are on your on, you can improve your control simply by hitting the ball against a wall and controlling it when it comes rebounding back to you. Otherwise, get a friend to throw the ball at you at different heights and practise using your chest, thigh and feet to control it as quickly and effectively as possible. Another method is to simply pass the ball between you, making sure you control it before passing back.

PASSING

SKILL School

PLAY LIKE THE STARS

TIP FROM THE STARS

"When you are playing at the top level, you must maintain possession of the ball. Good passing is vital for that to happen."

JAMIE REDKNAPP

WHAT PART OF THE FOOT DO YOU USE?

Usually the inside of your foot. Start by using that part anyway. Keep your head down and just gently move the ball towards your friend. When you have cracked that, try the outside of your foot but start off only a few

yards apart because it is harder to control the direction and pace of a pass with the outside of your foot.

WHAT ABOUT PASSING OVER A LONG DISTANCE?

You would use the area on your boot by your laces to do this - it's called the instep. And you need a bit more power as well, to make the ball travel further without being intercepted by an opponent. Strike through the ball like you do when shooting and raise your head as you make contact, leaning back a bit as you do to get height if you want the ball to go over another player's head.

HOW DO YOU PRACTISE?

Again, you can practise passing the ball against a wall. Or pass the ball backwards and forwards to a friend. Put down two markers and pass between them to your friend, moving further away as you get better.

TACKLING

DON'T YOU GET HURT TACKLING?

Only if you don't know how to do it properly or you go in half-heartedly, because you are scared of getting hurt. Tackling is an important part of the game and is vital in winning the ball for your team. But it is nothing to be scared of.

HOW DO YOU DO IT PROPERLY THEN?

There are different forms of tackling but the most common is 'block' tackling, which is when two players compete for the ball. Look at the picture and you can see how the two players have gone in from either side of the ball. That is a block tackle, they are both blocking the ball's path. When you are making a tackle, you must put your full weight into it.

Andy Cole

Shooting Stars

Dublin on goals

"Scoring goals is my business now, but that hasn't always been the case. I used to play in central defence, and still occasionally fill in at the back if needed. I have played in the Fourth, Third, Second and First Division and now I am playing in the Premiership and for England, so I really appreciate being at the top. My big break came when I signed for Man United and scored on my debut - but a broken leg finished my time there and Coventry gave me my next chance. Now I'm hoping for more goals and glory with Villa."

Fab Four

FEBRUARY 27, 1990 ABBEY STADIUM Cambridge 5 Bristol C. 1
Scored twice to help Cambridge to their record FA Cup victory in this Fifth Round second replay. The Fourth Division side reached the Quarter-Finals before being knocked out.
AUGUST 24, 1992 THE DELL Southampton 0 Man United 1
Dion silenced the critics, who said he'd never make it at United, as he celebrated his Red Devils' debut by scoring the only goal of the game, sliding the ball in from close range.
NOVEMBER 14, 1998 THE DELL Southampton 1 Aston Villa 4
In only his second match for Villa - having scored a double on his debut against Spurs - the striker grabbed a hat-trick.
DECEMBER 13, 1998 VILLA PARK Aston Villa 3 Arsenal 2
Dublin sparked an amazing second-half comeback against the double-winners. He fired home from Alan Thompson's miss-hit shot to level the scores at 2-2 and then pounced at a corner to score a dramatic winner.

DATAFILE

Name: Dion Dublin
Born: 22nd April, 1969 in Leicester
Height: 6ft 2in
Weight: 12st 4lb
Position: Striker
Other clubs played for:
Norwich City, Cambridge Utd, Man United, Coventry City

Score chart

CLUB	LGE GAMES	GOALS
Norwich	-	-
Cambridge	156	52
Man Utd	12	2
Coventry	145	61
A. Villa	24	11

Dion Dublin
Shooting Stars

Another Villa goal legend

DWIGHT YORKE

WHAT THE SAME ONE THAT IS AT MAN UNITED NOW?
That's him. Dwight was very popular at Villa Park and had top scored for three seasons running before he left early last term.

WHERE DID HE COME FROM?
Villa signed him for just £120,00 from a club called Signal Hill in Tobago back in the summer of 1989. He scored 44 goals in 164 League games for them and helped them to the 1994 League Cup before joining Man United for a whopping £12.6 million!

AND HE'S DONE PRETTY WELL AT UNITED TOO...
Definitely. Dwight's partnership with Andy Cole made them probably the best pair in the Premiership last season and also took United to the European Cup Final. Not bad!

DATAFILE

Name: Benito Carbone
Born: 14th August, 1971
in Italy
Height: 5ft 6in
Weight: 10st 8lb
Position: Striker
Other clubs played for: Torino (twice), Reggina, Casert, Ascoli, Napoli, Inter Milan (all Italy)

Benito Carbone
Shooting Stars

Score chart

CLUB	LGE GAMES	GOALS
Torino, Italy	8	-
Reggina, Italy	31	5
Casert, Italy	31	4
Ascoli, Italy	28	6
Torino, Italy	28	3
Napoli, Italy	29	5
Inter Milan, Italy	32	2
Sheff Wed	89	23

Another Owls goal legend

MARK BRIGHT

WHERE IS HE NOW?
After a long career as a strike partner to people like Gary Lineker and Ian Wright, Mark retired from football at the end of last season. His final season was spent in the Premiership with Charlton.

DID HE ACHIEVE MUCH?
His glory days were probably with Crystal Palace, who he and Wright helped to promotion to the top flight in 1989 and the FA Cup Final the following year.

WHAT ABOUT AT WEDNESDAY?
He netted 48 goals in 133 games for The Owls following his £1.375 million transfer from Palace in September 1992. He topped the club's scoring charts in 1994-95 with 13. These days he appears on The Big Breakfast on Channel 4.

Carbone on goals

"I'm very happy in Sheffield and that helps to give me the confidence to score goals. I was a bit unhappy in England at the start of last season and I also had a bad ankle injury, but the manager, Danny Wilson, persuaded me to stay and I'm pleased that I did. I like to entertain the fans and to score goals - that is very important to me. Now I want to get into the Italy team. I've represented my country at other levels, and the newspapers are always talking about me, so hopefully my chance will come."

Fab Four

NOVEMBER 18, 1996. HILLSBOROUGH. Sheff Wed 2 Nott'm For 0
In only his fourth game after a £3 million move from Inter Milan, Carbone netted his first goal for Wednesday. He pounced after 85 minutes to condemn Forest to defeat after Orlando Trustfull had given Wednesday the lead.

MARCH 5, 1997. CITY GROUND. Nott'm For 0 Sheff Wed 3
The Italian hit-man grabbed a spectacular double-strike to lift Wednesday into European contention while pushing the Nottingham club closer to the relegation places.

DECEMBER 9, 1998. HILLSBOROUGH. Sheff Wed 3 Nott'm For 2
Forest must feel Carbone has a curse over them. In this critical relegation battle, the silky skilled wide man struck two brilliant goals from long range to steer his team to victory.

APRIL 5, 1999. GOODISON PARK. Everton 1 Sheff Wed 2
Benito made Everton's careless defence pay for two mistakes with a couple of clinical finishes to make The Owls all but safe from relegation worries.

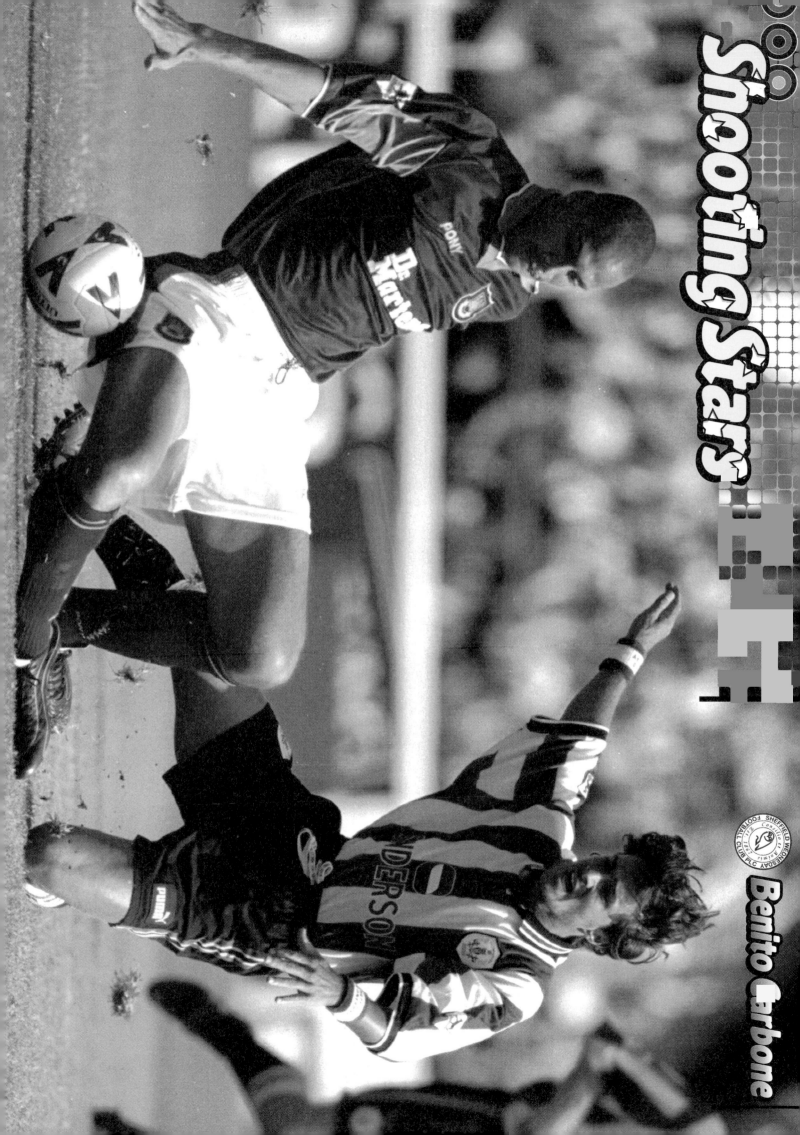

Shooting Stars

Benito Carbone

Shooting Stars!

Paulo Wanchope

DERBY COUNTY

Wanchope on goals

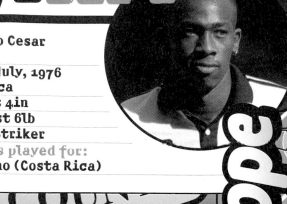

DATAFILE

Name: Paulo Cesar Wanchope
Born: 31st July, 1976 in Costa Rica
Height: 6ft 4in
Weight: 12st 6lb
Position: Striker
Other clubs played for: CS Herediano (Costa Rica)

"I like scoring goals, but just playing in England is great for me as I've not been a professional footballer for too long. I used to be really keen on basketball, and I went to America to play, but it ended up being football where I made the grade. Some of the techniques I learned in basketball are also useful in football, though. The way you can shield the ball with your body and use your arms. But it is hitting the net that gives me the most joy."

Fab Four

APRIL 5, 1997...OLD TRAFFORD...Man Utd 2 Derby 3
You couldn't ask for a much bigger entrance than this. In his first game since moving from Costa Rica, Wanchope scored an amazing solo goal after a brilliant 40-yard dribble.
FEBRUARY 4, 1998...COSTA RICA...Costa Rica 7 Cuba 2
Paulo is a big star at home in Costa Rica too. He showed why in this Americas Gold Cup tie, as he netted four times to help his country to a famous victory.
MAY 10, 1998...PRIDE PARK...Derby 1 Liverpool 0
Wanchope always enjoys the big occasion. His strike after 63 minutes of this match was his 13th of the season - making him Derby's top scorer for 1997-98, his first full campaign.
MARCH 13, 1999...PRIDE PARK...Derby 3 Liverpool 2
Liverpool were the victims again as two goals in a devastating five minute spell from Wanchope lifted Derby into the top six.

Score chart

CLUB	LGE GAMES	GOALS
Derby Co	72	23

Another Derby goal legend

DEAN SAUNDERS

HE'S BEEN AROUND A BIT...
Certainly has! He began as an apprentice with Swansea in 1982 and since then he's played for Cardiff, Brighton, Oxford, Derby, Liverpool, Aston Villa, Galatasaray (Turkey), Nottingham Forest, Sheffield United and Benfica (Portugal). He's also found time to notch up 70-odd caps for Wales.

WHAT'S HIS STYLE?
Nippy and skilful, Dean scores them all - close range tap-ins, flying headers and long range blasts. In total he's notched up almost 200 League goals in his career and a few vital ones for Wales, too.

WHAT DID HE DO AT DERBY?
Well, in the three seasons he was there he top scored every time and was hugely popular with The Rams' fans.

Paulo Wanchope
Shooting Stars

Shooting Stars

Kevin Phillips

Phillips on goals

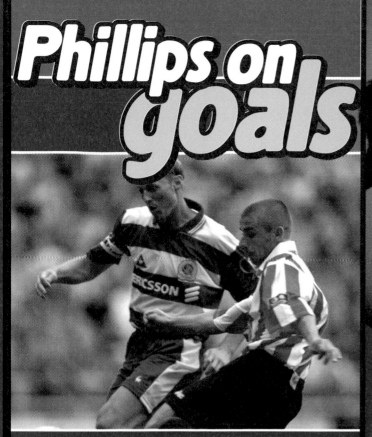

"The Sunderland fans were upset when I joined from Watford, because they were expecting a big name. But I'd scored goals in the First Division with Watford and I knew that I had what it takes to succeed. In a way that took the pressure off me a bit and the goals came easy once I got going. At Sunderland we play such attacking football that I get about six or seven chances a game - so I should be scoring plenty of goals. I usually set myself a target of 20 goals for a season - and I got a record-breaking 35 in my first year with Sunderland."

Fab Four

AUGUST 15, 1997...STADIUM OF LIGHT... Sunderland 3 Man City 1
King Kev celebrated his debut for Sunderland - and the first ever match at the new Stadium of Light - by scoring his opening goal for the club.
JANUARY 3, 1998...MILLMOOR... Rotherham 1 Sunderland 5
Poor old Rotherham found Phillips unstoppable in this FA Cup Third Round tie. The Sunderland striker notched up four of his side's five goals in a brilliant one-man show.
MARCH 28, 1998...STADIUM OF LIGHT... Sunderland 2 Bury 1
Phillips' 70th minute penalty set a new club record, with the striker having scored in nine consecutive home matches.
APRIL 13, 1999...GIGG LANE... Bury 2 Sunderland 5
Another four goal display from Phillips - taking his tally to 20 for the season - as Sunderland made sure of promotion to the Premiership with four games left.

DATAFILE

Name: Kevin Phillips
Born: 25th July, 1973, in Hitchin
Height: 5ft 7in
Weight: 11st
Position: Striker
Other clubs played for: Watford

Score chart

CLUB	LGE GAMES	GOALS
Watford	59	24
Sunderland	69	52

Another Sunderland goal legend

NIALL QUINN

WHAT'S HIS BACKGROUND?
Niall began his career with Arsenal and won the League Cup with them in 1987 before moving to Man City in March 1990. The Mackems paid £1.3m for him in August 1996.

AND EVERYTHING'S GONE WELL EVER SINCE?
Not at first. Quinn suffered three knee ops inside a year after joining Sunderland and for a spell thought his career might be over. But he has formed a fantastic partnership with Kevin Phillips, which led the club to the First Division Championship in 1998-99.

HOW DO THE PAIR WORK?
Niall is a big, strong 'old fashioned' forward. Although he's pretty good on the ground, his real strength is in the air and his flick-ons create loads of chances for Phillips.

Tony Cottee

DATAFILE

Name: Anthony Richard Cottee
Born: 11th July, 1965 in West Ham
Height: 5ft 8in
Weight: 11st 5lb
Position: Striker
Other clubs played for: West Ham (twice), Everton, Selangor (Malaysia), Birmingham (on loan)

Score chart

CLUB	LGE GAMES	GOALS
West Ham	212	92
Everton	184	72
West Ham	67	23
Birmingham	5	1
Leicester	50	14

Another Leicester goal legend

GARY LINEKER

ISN'T HE A TV PRESENTER?
He certainly is. But it's not so long ago that Gary was the best striker around. He scored a total of 48 goals for his country, making him the second best striker of all time in England matches.

WHAT ELSE?
Born and bred in Leicester Gary began his career at Filbert Street and scored 95 goals in 195 League games. He moved to Everton in July 1985 and scored 30 times in 41 matches before transferring to Barcelona. He later had spells with Tottenham and Japanese club Grampus 8.

HE MUST HAVE WON LOADS...
Surprisingly little. A Spanish Cup and the Euro Cup-Winners' Cup with Barcelona, and the FA Cup with Spurs. He also picked up two Footballer of the Year trophies (1986, 1992) and scored ten goals in the World Cup finals - a British record.

Cottee on goals

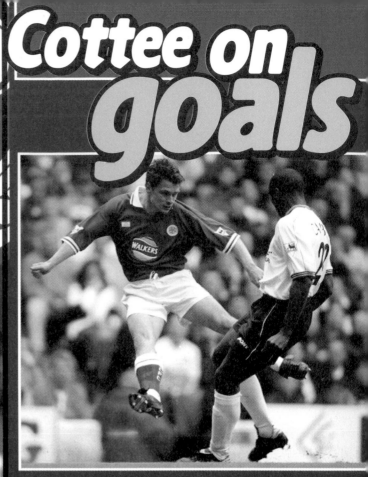

"I scored my 200th League goal last season - and I get as much pleasure from scoring today as I did in my early years. I love it. I've got a record of every goal I've ever scored. I used to keep all the newspaper clippings, but these days I keep stuff on video tape instead. I'm getting on a bit now, though, and I'm looking forward to having a go at a career in management before too long."

Fab Four

JANUARY 1, 1983 UPTON PARK West Ham 3 Tottenham 0
The 17-year-old Cottee made his debut at home to Tottenham - and introduced himself to The Hammers faithful with a goal, following up after Ray Clemence tipped a header onto the bar.
AUGUST 27, 1988 GOODISON PARK Everton 4 Newcastle 0
Having signed for a British record £2.3m in July 1988, Cottee was under pressure to live up to his star billing at Goodison Park. He made a bright start, with a hat-trick on his debut.
FEBRUARY 17, 1999 FILBERT STREET Leicester 1 Sunderland 1
In the second-leg of the Worthington Cup Semi-Final, Cottee scored after 54 minutes. Added to the two he had netted in the first-leg, his strike was enough to take Leicester to Wembley.
APRIL 3, 1999 WHITE HART LANE Tottenham 0 Leicester 2
When Cottee scored The Foxes' second after 67 minutes it wasn't just sweet revenge for their recent Worthington Cup Final defeat - it was also the 200th League goal of his career.

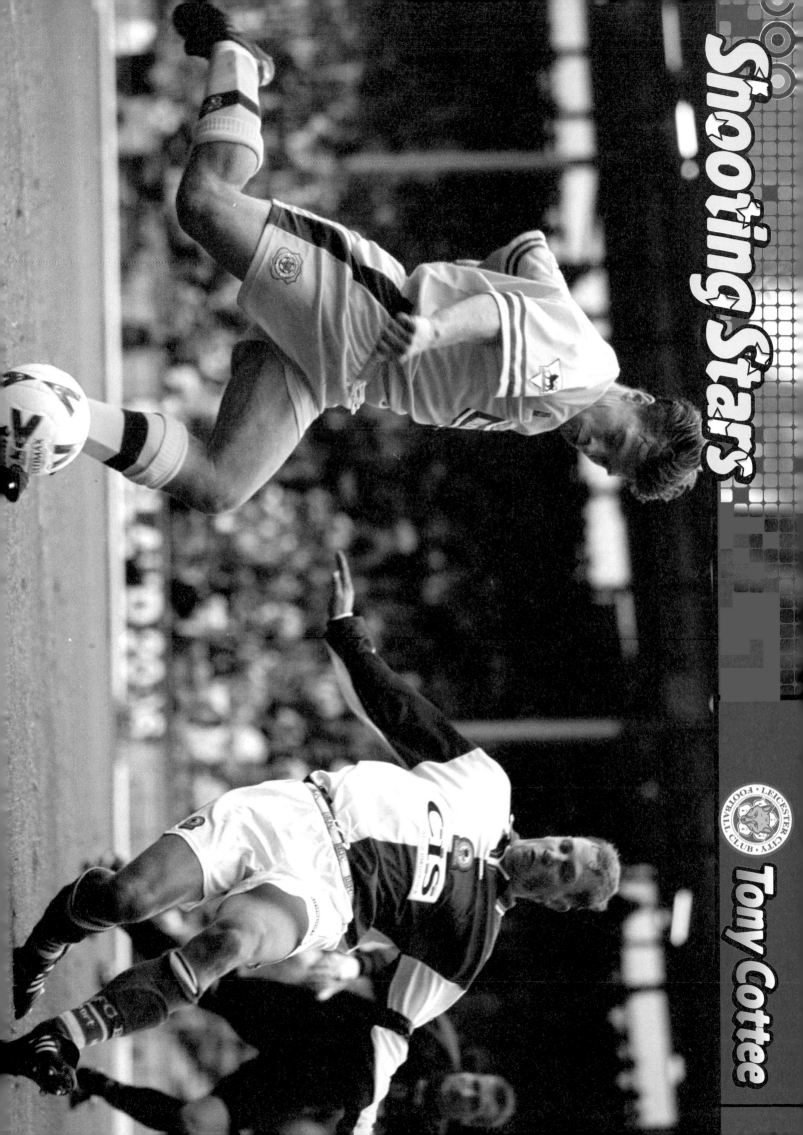

Tony Cottee

Quiz
What do you remember

THE ANSWERS TO THESE QUESTIONS CAN ALL BE FOUND IN OUR SHOOTING STARS SECTION.

1. WHO IS ANDY COLE'S NORMAL STRIKE PARTNER AT MAN UNITED?

2. AGAINST WHICH CLUB DID KEVIN PHILLIPS SCORE FOUR GOALS FOR SUNDERLAND LAST SEASON?

3. FOR WHICH CLUB DOES TONY COTTEE PLAY?

4. PAULO WANCHOPE IS AN INTERNATIONAL FOR COSTA RICA OR BRAZIL?

5. DION DUBLIN LEFT WHICH CLUB TO JOIN ASTON VILLA?

6. GIANFRANCO ZOLA USED TO PLAY FOR LIVERPOOL. TRUE OR FALSE?

SOCCER STARS
QUIZ Time No.5

Guessing Game

WE HAVE GIVEN YOU THREE ANSWERS TO EACH QUESTION. JUST CIRCLE THE CORRECT ONE.

1. WHO WON THE WORLD CUP IN 1998?
A) ENGLAND B) BRAZIL C) FRANCE

2. WHAT COLOURS DO SOUTHAMPTON NORMALLY WEAR?
A) RED AND WHITE STRIPES B) BLUE AND WHITE STRIPES C) ALL BLACK

3. WHERE DO CHELSEA PLAY ALL OF THEIR HOME GAMES?
A) OLD TRAFFORD B) STAMFORD BRIDGE C) UPTON PARK

4. WHO IS THE MANAGER OF TOTTENHAM?
A) KENNY DALGLISH B) HARRY REDKNAPP C) GEORGE GRAHAM

5. WHO WON THE FA CUP IN 1998?
A) ARSENAL B) MAN UNITED
C) NEWCASTLE

6. HOW MANY TIMES HAVE ENGLAND WON THE WORLD CUP?
A) 0 B) 1 C) 2

7. FOR WHICH COUNTRY DOES RYAN GIGGS PLAY INTERNATIONAL FOOTBALL?
A) ENGLAND B) SCOTLAND C) WALES

8. CELTIC'S HENRIK LARSSON PLAYS IN WHICH POSITION?
A) GOALKEEPER B) DEFENDER
C) STRIKER

9. HOW MANY PLAYERS IN A FOOTBALL TEAM?
A) 11 B) 10 C) 12

10. WHICH CLUB ARE NICKNAMED THE HAMMERS?
A) ASTON VILLA B) COVENTRY
C) WEST HAM

JumbLeD Up

OUR NAUGHTY DESIGNER HAS CUT UP PICTURES OF FOUR TOP STRIKERS AND JUMBLED THEM UP. CAN YOU SPOT WHO THEY ARE?

Colour 'em in

World Stars

SOCCER STARS

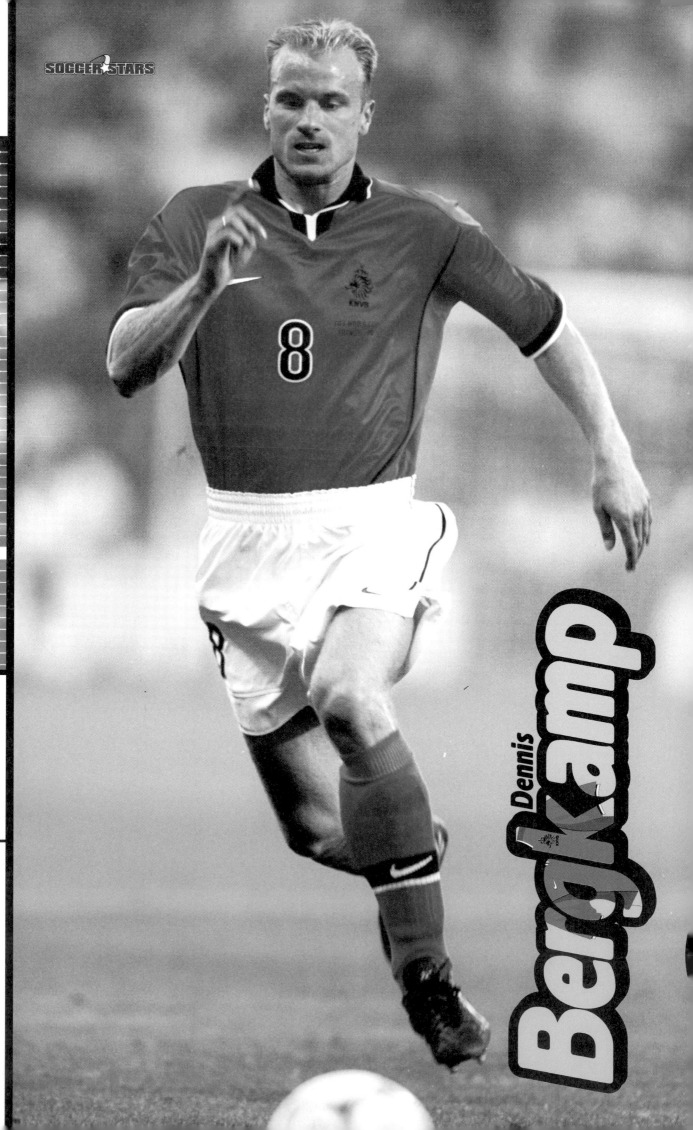

8

Dennis
BergKamp

World Stars

DATA FILE

Name: Dennis Bergkamp
Born: May 18th, 1969 in Amsterdam, Holland
Height: 6ft
Weight: 12st 5lb
Position: Striker
Clubs played for: Ajax Amsterdam (Holland), Inter Milan (Italy), Arsenal
Nickname: Bergy or Beavis
Normal shirt number: 10

WHO WAS YOUR HERO WHEN YOU WERE A BOY?

DENNIS SAYS: "Believe it or not, I followed Tottenham when I was young and my absolute hero was Glenn Hoddle. He was a brilliant player, with so much skill on the ball. I can't believe he didn't win more caps for England."

WE HEAR YOU ARE SCARED OF FLYING. WHAT'S THAT ALL ABOUT?

DENNIS SAYS: "I just can't do it - I don't really know why. I just know that flying terrifies me. I'm a bit disappointed that people keep talking about it. Arsenal have known about it for more than three years and have accepted it. Some players miss games through injury or suspension and in my case it is something else - flying."

YOU'VE PLAYED FOR AJAX AND INTER MILAN, HOW DO ARSENAL COMPARE WITH THEM AS ONE OF THE BIGGEST SIDES IN EUROPE?

DENNIS SAYS: "We're certainly getting there. We have Arsenal fans all over England, and the fan base is growing in Europe too. When you've got a few international players in the team, you grab the attention of supporters from those countries as well. For instance, in Holland we have many fans because of Marc Overmars and me, while the same thing is probably true in France with Manu Petit and Patrick Vieira here."

SO HOW DO YOU LIKE LIVING IN ENGLAND THEN?

DENNIS SAYS: "I feel like I'm almost an Englishman! My son and daughter were both born here and the family is very settled. My wife loves England and we can still get back to Holland when I play international matches. It is very close - only a train ride away."

HOW DO YOU GET SUCH BRILLIANT BALL CONTROL AND SKILL?

DENNIS SAYS: "Some of it is natural, but I've always believed that when you practise a lot with the ball then you reach a stage where you can do everything that you want. So my advice to youngsters is practise as much as you can with the ball."

FAMOUS TEAM-MATES

PATRICK KLUIVERT
HOLLAND

This young striker plays alongside Dennis in Holland's attack and is rated as one of the world's most exciting players. He was a star at World Cup 1998 in France and plays his club football for Spain's Barcelona.

MARC OVERMARS
ARSENAL

Bergkamp's room-mate and sidekick for club and country, Marc is one of the best wingers in the business. He's as fast as lightning and makes chances galore for his strikers, as well as scoring a fair few himself.

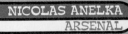

NICOLAS ANELKA
ARSENAL

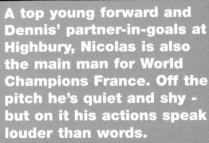

A top young forward and Dennis' partner-in-goals at Highbury, Nicolas is also the main man for World Champions France. Off the pitch he's quiet and shy - but on it his actions speak louder than words.

DATAFILE

Name: Ronaldo Luiz Nazario da Lima
Born: September 22nd, 1976 in Rio de Janeiro
Height: 6ft
Weight: 12st 1lb
Position: Striker
Clubs played for: Sao Cristovao, Cruzeiro (both Brazil), PSV Eindhoven (Holland), Barcelona (Spain), Inter Milan (Italy)
Nickname: The Golden One

FAMOUS TEAM-MATES

ROBERTO BAGGIO
INTER MILAN

The tricky striker played in three World Cup tournaments for Italy in 1990, 1994 and 1998, and became big friends with Ronaldo when the two teamed up at Inter last year. Labelled the 'best player in the world' in the mid-1990s.

DENILSON
BRAZIL

Took over from Ronaldo as the most expensive player in the world when he joined Real Betis in Spain for a cool £21 million after the 1998 World Cup. He has a wicked left foot and, along with Ronaldo, is seen as the golden future of Brazilian football.

ROBERTO CARLOS
BRAZIL

One of Ronaldo's best mates in footie, they share a hotel room when they are away with Brazil. Among the best defenders in the game, he takes a mean free-kick and once scored from 50 yards in a game for his team, Real Madrid.

What do you say... Ronaldo?

WHAT WERE YOU LIKE AT SCHOOL?

RONALDO SAYS: "Not very good, I'm afraid. I used to tell my mum I was going to school and then go and kick a ball about in the streets where I lived in Brazil. But I learnt so much from playing there. That is where loads of top footballers in the country started out - playing street football."

WHO WAS YOUR HERO WHEN YOU WERE YOUNG?

RONALDO SAYS: "A famous Brazilian called Zico. He played for my country many times and I have tried to copy some of his skills. He is a big hero with our fans even now."

HOW DOES IT FEEL TO BE THE BEST PLAYER IN THE WORLD?

RONALDO SAYS: "I don't think of myself in that way. I am a good player but that is all. It is nice to hear people calling me the best but I am more interested in helping my team to win trophies."

HOW DISAPPOINTED WERE YOU THAT BRAZIL DIDN'T WIN THE 1998 WORLD CUP IN FRANCE?

RONALDO SAYS: "I was ill before the Final against France and could not give my best in the match. I was very sorry about that because I dearly wanted to help my country win the World Cup. But the illness has gone now and maybe I will get another chance to win the Cup in the future."

WHAT IS IT LIKE PLAYING IN ITALY?

RONALDO SAYS: "It is a big challenge for me to be in Italy. It is very hard because the best defenders in the world play here, but in a way that makes it even more exciting. I've had a bad time with injuries over recent seasons. Hopefully it will be better next time."

soccer stars

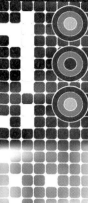

Ronaldo

BRAZIL | INTER MILAN

STRIKER

SOCCER STARS

STRIKER

ITALY
JUVENTUS

Alessandro
del Piero

What do you say...
del Piero

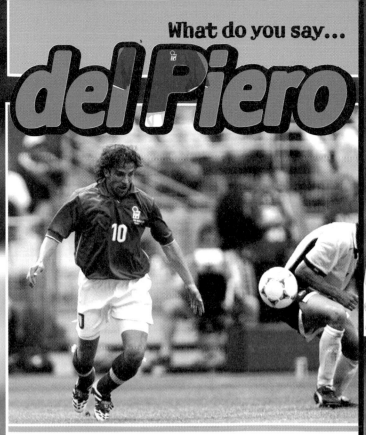

DATAFILE

Name: Alessandro del Piero
Born: November 9th, 1974 in Conegliano, Italy
Height: 5ft 7in
Weight: 11st
Position: Striker
Clubs played for: Padova, Juventus (both Italy)
Nickname: Alex
Normal shirt number: 10

WHO WAS YOUR HERO WHEN YOU WERE A YOUNG BOY?

DEL PIERO SAYS: "I used to love watching the French player Michel Platini, he was a genius with the ball. He used to play like an attacking midfielder and was always popping up to score wonderful goals."

WHEN YOU FIRST ARRIVED ON THE SCENE, PEOPLE WERE TALKING ABOUT YOU AS BEING THE WORLD'S BEST PLAYER, HOW DID THAT AFFECT YOU?

DEL PIERO SAYS: "I try to keep my feet on the ground. Thanks to the way my parents taught me I think I can handle fame in the right way."

WHAT ABOUT COMPARISONS BETWEEN YOU AND RONALDO?

DEL PIERO SAYS: "No, no. I do not want to compare myself with Ronaldo, nor even think about it. He is an excellent player, of course, but I have never considered one player to be important. Football is a team game and to talk so much about forwards is an insult to defenders."

YOU HAVE OFTEN BEEN LEFT OUT OF THE ITALY SIDE TO MAKE WAY FOR ROBERTO BAGGIO. HOW DOES THAT MAKE YOU FEEL?

DEL PIERO SAYS: "Italy have got plenty of high-quality players and we all have to fight for our place in the team, I understand that. I think I have shown good quality whenever I have played for the national side and I'm sure my time will come again. I am still only young."

EVERY TIME YOU HAVE A COUPLE OF BAD GAMES, PEOPLE ARE VERY QUICK TO CRITICISE YOU. WHAT DO YOU SAY TO THEM?

DEL PIERO SAYS: "People always seem to think I will struggle later because I have done well while still young. I don't want to be big-headed, but my record is there for all to see; the goals I've scored and the games I have won with Italy and Juventus."

FAMOUS TEAM-MATES

EDGAR DAVIDS
JUVENTUS

Known as 'The Pitbull' because of his tough-tackling, hard-running style, Juventus midfielder Davids was one of the outstanding players at World Cup 1998, when he starred for Holland in their run to the Semis.

FILIPPO INZAGHI
JUVENTUS

Alessandro and Inzaghi have a brilliant partnership at Juventus with del Piero so often the provider for Inzaghi's hunger for goals. Skilful and quick, Filippo is also a regular in the Italian national team.

CHRISTIAN VIERI
ITALY

The powerhouse Italian striker finished with five goals in World Cup 98 and that prompted Lazio to spend over £17 million to take him back to Serie A after his spell with Atletico Madrid.

DATAFILE

Name: Zinedine Zidane
Born: June 23rd, 1972 in Marseille, France
Height: 6ft 1in
Weight: 12st 6lb
Position: Midfield
Clubs played for: AS Cannes, Bordeaux (both France), Juventus (Italy)
Nickname: Zizou
Normal shirt number: 21 (Juventus), 10 (France)

FAMOUS TEAM-MATES

DIDIER DESCHAMPS
JUVENTUS & FRANCE

The captain of France's glorious World Cup winners and Zidane's midfield partner for club and country. A warrior in the centre of the field, Deschamps keeps everything ticking over and wins a lot of balls for his friend Zizou.

CHRISTOPHE DUGARRY
FRANCE

Zidane's best friend - on and off the pitch. The pair played together for France's Under-21s and for Bordeaux and enjoy a wonderful understanding on the pitch. They also jointly-own a restaurant and bar in Bordeaux.

PATRICK BARTHEZ
FRANCE

France's number one goalkeeper and the only man in the national team with less hair than Zidane. With brilliant reflexes, he loves to come to the edge of the box to take crosses. Like many 'keepers he's a bit crazy!

What do you say... Zidane?

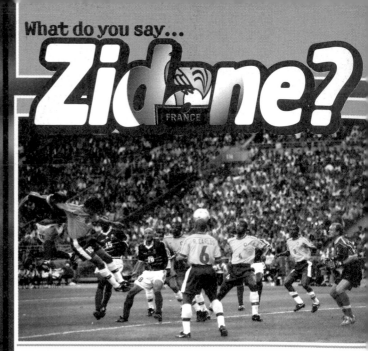

WHAT WAS IT LIKE WINNING THE WORLD CUP?

ZIDANE SAYS: "When we won I was so happy. Not just for me and my family, but for Laurent Blanc who couldn't play through suspension, for my sons Luca and Enzo, for my coaches, for the whole country. It was a wonderful feeling, I cannot describe it."

AND YOU SCORED TWO GOALS IN THE FINAL TOO...

ZIDANE SAYS: "Yes, they were two very important goals. I needed to score so much to make up to my team-mates for being so stupid as to get sent-off against Saudi Arabia the way I did. I had apologised, but I knew that wasn't enough. I had to give something back."

DO YOU THINK YOU WILL EVER PLAY IN ENGLAND?

ZIDANE SAYS: "The English League is very exciting and is full of wonderful players, but it is not one of my immediate aims to play in the Premiership. I would prefer to play in Spain if I was going to go anywhere. But I am under contract with Juventus until 2003 and I am very happy here."

ERIC CANTONA IS A FRENCH PLAYER WHO DID VERY WELL IN ENGLAND. WHAT DO YOU THINK OF HIM?

ZIDANE SAYS: "Eric was one of the best, most spectacular forwards you could hope to find. I played with him early in my career when he was captain of France and he was an excellent player; a good leader. Those who criticise Eric don't know him."

HOW DID IT FEEL TO BE VOTED EUROPEAN AND WORLD FOOTBALLER OF THE YEAR IN 1998?

ZIDANE SAYS: "It is strange to think that people rate me as the 'best player'. 1998 was an incredible year for me, full of success and big rewards. It's a great triumph for me, but it would have been impossible without the Juventus and French teams around me. I was lucky to play for two great sides and people always remember the winners."

SOCCER STARS

World Stars

Zinedine **Zidane**

FRANCE
JUVENTUS

MIDFIELDER

World Stars

soccerstars

ARGENTINA FIORENTINA

STRIKER

Gabriel **Batistuta**

What do you say...
Batistuta

DATAFILE

Name: Gabriel Batistuta
Born: February 1st, 1969 in Avellaneda, Argentina
Height: 6ft 1in
Weight: 11st 5lb
Position: Striker
Clubs played for: Newell's Old Boys, River Plate, Boca Juniors (all Argentina), Fiorentina (Italy)
Nickname: Batigol
Normal shirt number: 9

FAMOUS TEAM-MATES

YOU HAVE SCORED MORE GOALS IN *SERIE A* THAN ANY OTHER FOREIGNER. HOW WOULD YOU DESCRIBE YOURSELF AS A PLAYER?

BATISTUTA SAYS: "I never give up, I never tire of scoring goals and will never be satisfied with what I have achieved. For example, I never waste time thinking over the goals I have scored or the records I have set. What's important for me is the next goal I score, the next record. I always want to improve, to get better and to score more goals."

CAN YOU GET BETTER THEN?

BATISTUTA SAYS: "Of course, that is what I am aiming for. For instance, I need to improve my left foot shot and I train with that in mind. Nobody is perfect and you can always get better in some areas of your game."

HAVE YOU EVER THOUGHT ABOUT PLAYING IN ENGLAND?

BATISTUTA SAYS: "Once I have said goodbye to Florence I would like to play for at least one year in England. There are two reasons: first, because British football is exciting and you are always looking to score goals, second because it would allow me to perfect my English."

GETTING AWAY FROM FOOTBALL, DO YOU HAVE ANY FAMOUS FRIENDS OUTSIDE THE SPORT?

BATISTUTA SAYS: "Since playing in Italy I have met the Pope, which was one of my dreams. I am a believer and that meeting was very special for me. Also, the motor racing driver Michael Schumacher has been giving me flying lessons. I don't devote my entire life to football and learning to fly an aeroplane is a wonderful diversion for me."

FINALLY, GABRIEL, WHAT MESSAGE WOULD YOU GIVE TO YOUNG SOCCERSTARS READERS WHO WANT TO BECOME BETTER FOOTBALLERS?

BATISTUTA SAYS: "Play for enjoyment. Just think about playing - nothing else; not about millionaire contracts or fashionable clothes. Play football and enjoy football. That is by far the most important thing."

RUI COSTA
FIORENTINA

The brilliant playmaker of Fiorentina's 1998-99 Italian League Championship chasing side, Rui Costa is one of the world's best at opening up opposing defences. Also an established international with Portugal, the midfielder's passing helps make Batistuta tick in front of goal.

ARIEL ORTEGA
ARGENTINA

Argentina's brightest young star and the only current player close to taking over from the legendary Diego Maradona as his country's favourite footballer. He has bags of skill, is an expert passer of the ball and also scores some spectacular goals. A star at World Cup 1998 in France.

DIEGO SIMEONE
ARGENTINA

Former Argentina captain who is also a star for Inter Milan. Shot to fame at World Cup 1998 for his part in the incident which led to David Beckham's sending-off - but is also a fine marker and passer of the ball who creates many chances for Batigol.

Batistuta

DATAFILE

Name: Jaap Stam
Born: July 17th, 1972 in Kampen, Holland
Height: 6ft 3in
Weight: 14st
Position: Central Defender
Clubs played for: FC Zwolle, Cambuur Leeuwarden, Willem II Tilburg, PSV Eindhoven (all Holland), Man United
Nickname: Fester (uncle in the Addams Family)
Normal shirt number: 6

FAMOUS TEAM-MATES

DAVID BECKHAM
MANCHESTER UNITED

Like Stam, Beckham starred in the 1998 World Cup and has since enjoyed great times at Old Trafford. One of the best crossers of the ball in the world, he is also deadly from free-kicks around the box and was wicked last season.

DWIGHT YORKE
MANCHESTER UNITED

Relieved Stam of the title of United's 'most expensive player' when he signed for more than £12 million during the 1998-99 season. A fantastic finisher who always plays with a big smile on his face.

FRANK DE BOER
HOLLAND

Stam's partner in the heart of the Dutch defence and national team skipper. He is one of the most skilful defenders in the game, hits a wicked pass, long or short and works perfectly alongside his awesome sidekick.

What do you say... Stam

WHAT MADE YOU DECIDE TO COME AND PLAY IN ENGLAND?

STAM SAYS: "You always want to prove yourself as a player and to do that as a defender you have to play against the best strikers in the world. Most of them play in England, so that is why I came here. It is also good fun playing in England at the moment - every team tries to win, and that is very impressive. I like that very much."

WHICH STRIKERS HAVE YOU BEEN MOST IMPRESSED WITH THEN?

STAM SAYS: "I have found every striker I have come across in England a tough customer, but I would say that Nicolas Anelka has been the hardest. He has great pace and is a good player as well. The runs he makes are so hard to stop and that makes him very dangerous."

DID YOUR TRANSFER FEE WORRY YOU?

STAM SAYS: "It was a lot of money at £10 million but I am used to it now. Most clubs are paying big money for all kinds of players nowadays so the price tag isn't so important any more. Anyway, soon after I arrived Dwight Yorke turned up - and he cost a lot more than me!"

YOU HAD THE CHANCE TO COME OVER SEVERAL YEARS AGO, WHEN SHEFFIELD WEDNESDAY TRIED TO SIGN YOU. WHY DID YOU TURN THEM DOWN?

STAM SAYS: "I came over on trial with Sheffield Wednesday, but I felt out of place playing against people like Trevor Francis and Chris Waddle. They wanted to sign me, but I decided to stay in Holland. At the time I still lived with my parents and had never even been abroad before. It all happened too soon for me then."

THERE ARE LOTS OF GREAT PLAYERS AT MAN UNITED - WHO DO YOU THINK WILL BE THE NEXT SUPERSTAR?

STAM SAYS: "A young defender called Wes Brown has really impressed me. I saw him play against Leeds before I signed for United and he looked very good. Now I have played alongside him and I know he is good! I'm sure he will play regularly for England."

SOCCER STARS

World Stars

Jaap
Stam

HOLLAND
MAN UNITED

DEFENDER

World Stars

SOCCER STARS

MIDFIELDER

FRANCE
ARSENAL

Emmanuel **Petit**

What do you say...

Petit

DATAFILE

Name: Emmanuel Petit
Born: September 22nd,
1970 in Dieppe, France
Height: 6ft 1in
Weight: 12st 7lb
Position: Midfield
Clubs played for: ES Arques,
AS Monaco (both France), Arsenal
Nickname: Manu
Normal shirt number: 17

THE 1998 SEASON WAS A PRETTY SPECIAL ONE FOR YOU - HAS IT AFFECTED YOUR DESIRE TO KEEP WINNING TROPHIES?

PETIT SAYS: "No, not at all. You can never have enough of winning at football. My desire to have success is still as strong as ever and we are all determined to keep doing well. Playing against the best teams and players is a challenge on its own."

YOU HAD SOME PROBLEMS IN YOUR EARLY DAYS IN THE FRENCH TEAM, DIDN'T YOU?

PETIT SAYS: "I was first selected for France when I was just 19-years-old, and I let myself down a little bit by not working hard enough. It took me some time to realise that I had to work at my game, listen to the advice I was getting and always give 100 per cent - in training as well as in matches."

HAS WINNING THE WORLD CUP WITH FRANCE CHANGED YOU?

PETIT SAYS: "I guess it has in a way, yes. The French people now treat us as heroes and that is a big responsibility for the players to carry. We have to watch our attitude and our behaviour because we are role models to the French youngsters. We must not set a bad example. I am proud to be in that position, though."

HOW DO YOU COPE WITH ALL OF THE HYPE AND PRESSURE OF BEING A FOOTBALL SUPERSTAR?

PETIT SAYS: "I actually prefer to be under pressure, rather than just play an easy game. I think it gets the best out of me to be in that situation. For example, playing for Arsenal in front of 40,000 fans: you want to succeed for them. I relish the challenge."

WHAT DOES THE FUTURE HOLD FOR YOU?

PETIT SAYS: "I have promised myself that I will never be lazy again. I will continue to work at my game and to look after myself like every professional should. I paid the price for not doing that before, and I learnt an important lesson."

FAMOUS TEAM-MATES

PATRICK VIEIRA
ARSENAL & FRANCE

Manu's team-mate and room-mate for both Arsenal and France. An excellent reader of the game with top passing skills and a crunching tackle his partnership with Petit did much to guide Arsenal to the League and FA Cup 'double' in 1998.

THIERRY HENRY
FRANCE

A club mate of Petit's at Monaco in France, teenager Henry burst onto the international scene at World Cup 1998 when he was one of the players of the tournament. Looks sure to have a bright future with several leading clubs trying to sign him.

YOURI DJORKAEFF
FRANCE

The Inter Milan striker was one of many French stars who lit up Wembley in February 1999 as England were beaten 2-0. Played his part in his country's World Cup success and is great friends with Manu.

DATAFILE

Name: Rivaldo Vitor Borba Ferreira
Born: April 19th, 1972 in Recife, Brazil
Height: 6ft 1in
Weight: 11st 6lb
Position: Striker
Clubs played for: Santa Cruz, Mogi Mirim, Corinthians, Palmeiras (all Brazil), Deportivo La Coruna, Barcelona (both Spain)
Normal shirt number: 11 (Barcelona) 10 (Brazil)

FAMOUS TEAM-MATES

LUIS ENRIQUE
BARCELONA

One of the best Spanish players around and a regular in their national team for years. Versatile, he can play at wing-back or in his more preferred attacking position and links up well with Rivaldo down the flanks. One of the real heroes of the Barcelona and Spain fans.

SONNY ANDERSON
BARCELONA

Rivaldo's front-running partner at Barcelona. The dynamic duo netted 29 goals in their first season together (1997-98) and they gave Man United problems in the Champions' League last term with Anderson scoring once and Rivaldo twice the 3-3 draw at the Nou Camp.

JUNINHO
BRAZIL

Missed out on the World Cup with Brazil because of injury but back in the national team picture now. Came up through the ranks with Rivaldo in the yellow shirt. Middlesbrough fans will remember his silky skills in the two years he was at the Riverside club.

What do you say...
Rivaldo?

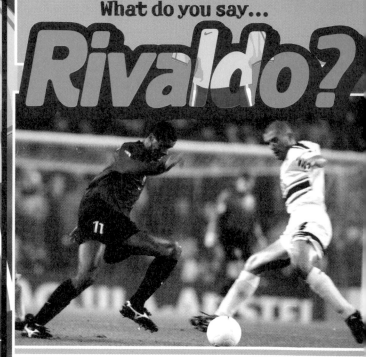

DO YOU WATCH MUCH ENGLISH FOOTBALL IN SPAIN?

RIVALDO SAYS: "It is on quite a lot on television. I like watching Premiership matches and it is good to see that the skilful side of the game is improving in England. English football has always been famous for the fighting spirit and physical power in the air and on the ground but now there is a lot of skill involved as well."

WHAT DID YOU THINK OF MANCHESTER UNITED AFTER PLAYING THEM IN THE CHAMPIONS' LEAGUE LAST SEASON?

RIVALDO SAYS: "They are a great team, for sure. We had two magnificent matches against them last season and they are very attack-minded. With players like Yorke, Cole, Beckham, Giggs and Scholes, they couldn't be any other way."

WHAT IS YOUR BIG AMBITION AT BARCELONA THEN?

RIVALDO SAYS: "To win the Champions' League. We have failed to make it past the group stage in our last two attempts and that is very disappointing. Last season we were in a very strong group with Manchester United, Bayern Munich and Brondby. It was very hard for us but we did not win our important home games. That was our trouble."

HOW DISAPPOINTED WERE YOU NOT TO WIN THE WORLD CUP WITH BRAZIL?

RIVALDO SAYS: "It was a big blow to our country and to all the players. We played some beautiful football in the tournament but not in the Final against France. Always, Brazil players try to entertain our fans but in that game we were very disappointing and were sorry for all our supporters."

WE HEAR THAT YOU DON'T GET ON WITH RONALDO. IS THAT REALLY TRUE?

RIVALDO SAYS: "Not at all. He is a fantastic player and everyone knows how much we missed a fit Ronaldo in the Final. People tried to build up a rivalry between us during the World Cup but it does not exist. We might not be best friends but we are not enemies."

World Stars

Rivaldo

BRAZIL
BARCELONA

STRIKER

Quiz

What do you remember

THE ANSWERS TO THESE QUESTIONS CAN ALL BE FOUND IN OUR WORLD STARS SECTION.

1. DENNIS BERGKAMP HAS A FEAR OF WHAT?

2. HOW MANY GOALS DID ZINEDINE ZIDANE SCORE IN THE 1998 WORLD CUP FINAL?

3. FOR WHICH COUNTRY DOES ALESSANDRO DEL PIERO PLAY - ITALY OR SPAIN?

4. RONALDO NORMALLY WEARS WHAT NUMBER SHIRT?

5. EMMANUEL PETIT JOINED ARSENAL FROM MANCHESTER UNITED. TRUE OR FALSE?

6. IN WHICH POSITION DOES JAAP STAM PLAY?

SOCCER★STARS

QUIZ Time No.6

Link 'em up

BELOW ARE THE FLAGS AND STRIPS OF SIX OF THE WORLD'S BEST NATIONAL SIDES. JUST LINK THEM UP BY DRAWING A LINE FROM THE BADGE TO THE MATCHING STRIP.

WORDSEARCH

Hidden in the giant wordsearch are the names of 20 world stars. They can be found in the grid below vertically, horizontally, diagonally or even backwards. We've found the first one for you. Can you spot the rest?

Nicolas ANELKA Roberto BAGGIO Gabriel BATISTUTA Dennis BERGKAMP DENILSON Marcel DESAILLY David GINOLA Paul INCE Ariel ORTEGA Marc OVERMARS RIVALDO RONALDO Peter SCHMEICHEL Alan SHEARER Ole Gunnar SOLSKJAER Jaap STAM Davor SUKER Christian VIERI Zinedine ZIDANE Gianfranco ZOLA

G	I	N	O	L	A	P	R	D	L	S	T	A	M	T	S
A	T	O	D	K	I	M	C	E	A	C	C	M	F	H	O
E	A	K	L	E	N	A	E	A	M	H	M	B	D	F	L
C	W	I	A	X	L	K	E	B	P	M	A	C	E	Y	S
H	M	E	N	O	N	G	N	R	A	E	Z	E	R	M	K
T	T	P	O	I	U	R	S	E	R	I	N	C	E	D	J
M	C	A	R	R	E	E	L	L	D	C	S	A	W	A	A
A	L	O	Z	R	T	B	K	A	E	H	E	B	P	O	E
T	S	M	A	R	S	E	N	R	S	E	K	E	R	I	R
U	E	E	A	Y	R	E	G	R	A	L	R	K	E	I	M
T	H	E	D	I	A	N	N	A	I	O	O	Y	V	N	U
S	U	K	E	R	M	I	E	R	L	O	Y	A	Y	O	R
I	R	E	I	V	R	G	H	B	L	I	L	H	E	U	T
T	R	Y	O	Y	E	G	P	U	Y	D	N	W	O	O	O
A	E	T	O	P	V	L	U	T	O	R	E	O	R	T	M
B	A	G	G	I	O	P	E	N	O	S	L	I	N	E	D

Colour 'em in

QUIZ answers

QUIZ 1

What do you remember: 1. Aston Villa. 2. Yes. 3. Louise. 4. Newcastle. 5. False, it was 1991. 6. Norway. **Link 'em up:** Badges top to bottom are: Sheff Wed; Derby; Everton; Wimbledon; Chelsea; Tottenham. Kits are: Wimbledon; Chelsea; Tottenham; Derby; Everton; Sheff Wed.

QUIZ 2

What do you remember: 1. Everton. 2. Borussia Dortmund. 3. True. 4. Posh. 5. Rugby League. 6. Nottingham Forest.

Spot the difference: Alan Shearer's shorts are red; Polish player's socks are yellow; ball missing; goalie's hand missing; Sainsbury's advert upside down. **Who am I?** 1. Paul Scholes. 2. Dennis Bergkamp.

QUIZ 3

What do you remember: 1. Republic of Ireland. 2. Leeds. 3. Dwight Yorke. 4. Crazy. 5. Nigel Martyn. 6. Shaka Hislop. **Who beat the goalie?** 2. **Identity Parade:** 1. Ronaldo. 2. Tore Andre Flo. 3. Alan Shearer. 4. Darren Anderton. 5. Jamie Redknapp. 6. Jimmy Floyd Hasselbaink. 7. Rio Ferdinand. 8. Jaap Stam. 9. Michael Owen.

QUIZ 4

What do you remember: 1. Midfield. 2. Yes. 3. Man United. 4. Old Trafford. 5. No. 6. David O'Leary. **Missing clubs:** : Ince - West Ham; Shearer - Blackburn; Cole - Newcastle; Ferdinand - QPR; Wright - Arsenal.

You've been framed: Di Matteo now Matte; 'S' on shirt wrong way around; Flo's shorts green; Flo's hair orange; Flo's shirt has Man United badge.

QUIZ 5

What do you remember: 1. Dwight Yorke. 2. Bury. 3. Leicester. 4. Costa Rica. 5. Coventry. 6. False. **Guessing Game:** 1) c; 2) a; 3) b; 4) c; 5) a; 6) b; 7) c; 8) c; 9) a; 10) c. **Jumbled up:** Top left: Dwight Yorke; Top right: Tore Andre Flo; Bottom left: Nicolas Anelka; Bottom right: David Ginola.

QUIZ 6

What do you remember: 1. Flying. 2. 2. 3. Italy. 4. Nine. 5. False. 6. Defender. **Link 'em up:** Flags top to bottom are: Romania; Italy; Spain; England; Germany; Brazil. Kits are: Spain; Brazil; Germany; Italy; England; Romania.

```
J H B O W Y E R E L W O F
O T O R K I A C E A L C M
A V V H E L C E A M A M B
C W I S X L L E B P M A C
H M E E O N O N R A S H E
I T P A I U C S E R T E P
M C A M P R R L L O N S A
A O O A P E A K A Y G E Y
M S M N R S L A R J T K E
D E R A Y G O E R T E R K
F E E D I N N N D S O O S
S H L S K J I E R T O Y E
S H E R I N G H A M I Y H
```

```
G I N O L A P R D L S T A M T S
A T O D K I M C E A C C M F H O
E A K L E N A E A M H M B D F L
C W I A X L K E B P M A C E Y S
H M E N O N G N R A E Z E R M K
T T P O I U R S E R I N C E D J
M C A R R E E L L D C S A W A A
A L O Z R T B K A E H E B P O E
T S M A R S E N R S E K E R I R
U E E A Y R E G R A L R K E I M
T H E D I A N N A I O O Y V N U
S U K E R M I E R L O Y A Y O R
I R E I V R G H B L I L H E U T
T R Y O Y E G P U Y D N W O O O
A E T O P V L U T O R E O R T M
B A G G I O P E N O S L I N E D
```